PRAISE FOR *BREADCRUMBS FROM SPIRIT*

In the pages of this beautiful book, *Breadcrumbs from Spirit,* Brandi offers a deeply authentic and uplifting journey about healing and remembrance. Her courage to embody her light will inspire countless souls to step into their own. Brandi walks the path of unity consciousness with humility and grace, inviting us all to embody the divine light within. This book is a gift for anyone ready to lead their lives from a space of unwavering love.

~Emmanuel Dagher,
Best Selling Author, Holistic Therapist

Reading this book feels like being gently led back to your own heart. Brandi invites us into her sacred journey of healing with such raw, vulnerable honesty that you cannot help but recognize pieces of yourself within her story. She courageously opens the door to wounds many of us carry—wounds often buried under layers of shame, fear, and silence. With openness and grace, she exposes the deeper places of generational pain that so often live unseen within us, quietly shaping our patterns, our relationships, and our daily lives.

What makes this work extraordinary is how she doesn't leave us in the heaviness of those truths. With wisdom and compassion, she weaves in spiritual teachings that stretch the mind and open the heart, showing us that healing is not only possible, it is our birthright.

She reminds us that Spirit is always for us—always moving, always whispering, always guiding us back to the truth of who we are.

This book is more than a memoir. It is an invitation to remember that we are not alone in our pain, and that even the most hidden suffering can be met with love, transformed through grace, and reclaimed as a deeper knowing of our worth and belonging. It is a sacred companion for anyone who longs to break free from the patterns of the past and step courageously into the fullness of their own soul.

~Kate Shipp, C-IAYT
Authentic Life Strategist and Holistic Trauma Specialist

Breadcrumbs from Spirit is a vulnerable and courageous invitation to walk beside Brandi on a journey of healing, awakening, and profound self-discovery with the goal of inspiring the reader to do the same. Her voice is a true guide for anyone seeking meaning, connection, and a deeper sense of purpose and peace.

~Jennifer J.

The author displays and by example teaches a great degree of humility. She has an openness that allows her to learn from broader realities than the vast majority of humanity has access to.

Her view captures a broad range of spiritual wisdom and understanding. She has clearly done the deep work necessary to ascend that path.

She uses the phrase BUT/AND to step back and transcend simple black and white interpretations. By doing so, she exemplifies higher levels of unified consciousness that lie beyond the duality that most of us live.

Kudos for such an exquisite work. I intend to read it again and again, as it is clearly a sentinel work that can teach you more and more each time you read it.

~Robert D. Sheeler, M.D.

Brandi is a delightful person who, in this book, teaches you how to transcend the places you are stuck. By sharing her own struggles and eventual victory over illness and past trauma, she demonstrates how the common culture is a distraction that keeps us stuck.

Using a variety of techniques from breath work to spiritual discipline, she has identified and remediated many areas of her life. By sharing such intimate detail, she shows the spectrum of what is possible to accomplish.

If you seek peace, understanding, growth, forgiveness, and love on a higher level, I would highly recommend this book.

~Angela E. O'Neil, M.D.
Fmr Assistant Dean, Mayo Clinic Medical School

This book, page by page, exemplifies Brandi's authenticity and takes us along on her journey to self-love. While I may have witnessed this evolution, her storytelling is relatable and relevant, with lessons attached along the way, and a few surprises! She speaks into her trauma with such vulnerability that you ache for her and ultimately cheer for her. She highlights the importance of finding your community, finding your people, as you are finding your way. This book transcends lines of spirituality and will absolutely resonate with anyone as they navigate their own path of growth and self-love.

~Kristi Ward, M.Ed.
Fmr Division Director, Maricopa County Adult Probation

I started reading this from the perspective that it was a book about spirituality, and what I experienced is that it is a book about becoming whole with yourself ... your own best friend. Brandi's life experiences and story are inspiring as well as instructive for living your best life.

~Karie Montague, LPC
Vistage CEO and Women Presidents Chair

Breadcrumbs from Spirit

A MEMOIR OF HEALING, SPIRITUAL AWAKENING, AND THE JOURNEY TO WHOLENESS

BRANDI STRIETER

Book Design by Transcendent Publishing | TranscendentPublishing.com
Editing by Mary Rembert and Dana Micheli
Author Photography by Hannah Lorsch/Slate Media Creative

The content of this book is for informational purposes only and is not intended to diagnose, treat, cure, or prevent any condition or disease. You understand that this book is not intended as a substitute for consultation with a licensed practitioner.

Printed in the United States of America.

For Dax

My faithful companion, guardian, and healer.

Thank you for walking beside me through the darkest nights and the brightest awakenings. You held space for me in silence when I couldn't find the words. You grounded me with your steady presence, teaching me how to return to my body, to the moment, and to love without condition.

Your eyes always saw the truth of me, even when I couldn't.

You were more than a dog. You were soul family, an anchor, and a teacher. This book carries the imprint of your love, quietly guiding each step of my unfolding.

I carry you with me, always.

Forever grateful.

Forever changed.

TABLE OF CONTENTS

FOREWORD

I still remember the first time Brandi sat across from me. She had just lost her mom, and her grief was raw, her body was overwhelmed, and her spirit was crying for attention. Yet, her eyes told a different story—one of pain, yes, but also possibility. I could see it, and, more importantly, I could feel it: that spark of light within, that deep soul wisdom just waiting to be awakened. Brandi had a quiet knowing that even though she didn't have it all figured out, she was ready to say yes to *something*. She didn't know where the path would lead—she just knew she couldn't stay where she was.

Over the years, I've had the privilege of guiding and supporting thousands of people on their spiritual journey, and from that very first session, I knew Brandi's journey would be powerful, not just for her, but for the people she would one day help. I saw her as a teacher, in her full power.

And now, here we are, full circle. Brandi is no longer a woman sitting across from me, searching for herself. She's a part of my team. She's a gifted teacher. She's a woman who has embodied her Light and shares it in the most authentic way. Walking alongside her over the past eight years has been an honor; her transformation has been one of the most inspiring I've witnessed.

Brandi did what so many people talk about doing but few actually commit to: she showed up for herself, again and again, even when it was hard ... *especially* when it was hard. She opened up. She did the work. She fell and got back up stronger—and softer—every time. I've watched her cry the tears, celebrate the breakthroughs, and reclaim her body as a sacred vessel, rather than a problem to be solved. I saw her release the weight—physically, emotionally, and energetically. I saw her mind shift from fear and self-doubt to clarity and confidence. I felt her connection to Spirit deepen, not just as a daily checklist, but as a true relationship with the Divine that guided her healing journey every step of the way. I watched her claim her power and step into her role as a teacher.

And, most reverently, I have had the opportunity to watch her write this book! And THIS book ... WOW!!! *Breadcrumbs from Spirit* is a memoir, yes, and it is so much more than that. It's a sacred offering. A guide. A permission slip. A hand to hold onto when you need one the most. It's everything Brandi learned, lived, let go of, and leaned into; it's a trail of light for those who are ready to come home to themselves, their truth, their power ... their healing.

Brandi's journey reminds us that healing is not a straight line, and it's not meant to be walked in isolation. The mind needs support. The body needs love. The spirit needs remembrance. And the heart needs connection with others, safety, and witnessing. She found those things, and now she offers them to you.

This story is about returning to self, to soul, to love. It's about the power of community, the strength of vulnerability, and the courage to ask for help when everything inside you wants to hide.

If you've ever felt like your body was betraying you, your mind was working against you, or your family didn't understand ... if you've felt disconnected from Spirit, or stuck in the stories that say, "I can't heal," *Breadcrumbs from Spirit* is for you.

Healing is not a destination. It's a way of living, a way of loving yourself through the mess and the miracle. Let Brandi's words remind you of your own power, and of just how miraculous, worthy, and holy you already are. Let her story show you what's possible when you stop trying to do it all alone and start letting yourself be supported.

I couldn't be prouder of Brandi, and I couldn't be more excited for you. Why? Because if you're holding this book, your journey to wholeness has already begun.

So, take a breath with me. You're ready, and you don't have to do it alone. It's not easy, but it is worth it, my friend.

Turn the page …

With Deep Love & Light,
Sunny Dawn Johnston
Spiritual Teacher, Intuitive Guide, and Founder of the School of Light

INTRODUCTION

One afternoon in early 2025, I was driving home after having lunch with my son Billy. Just an average day in Phoenix—warm, sunny … and crazy traffic on the 101 freeway.

I was going a bit over the speed limit just trying to keep up with the other cars, but they were whizzing by me so fast on both sides that I might as well have been standing still. Then they started weaving between lanes, everyone trying to get an edge over the other.

This chaos was made worse by the fact that I rarely drive on the freeway these days. A feeling of stress crept over me, maybe even fear of an accident. After several minutes of white-knuckling the steering wheel and trying to have eyes everywhere at once, I called in my team of Light, my bubble of protection.

I'd done this countless times before, and, other than Archangel Michael, I didn't single out specific energies. The way I see it, whoever wants to come is welcome. That day, inspired by a recent class I had taken, I figured, what the heck?

Immediately, a frequency moved in beside me. I didn't see it with my eyes, but I felt it drop right into the passenger seat.

It wasn't something outside of me. It was something I recognized from within. A resonance. A presence. A knowing. It was an energy I had been connecting with for years.

Our conversation began something like this:

What the hell are you doing here? I'm on the 101! People are driving ninety miles an hour. I told you that I didn't want to get into an accident, and now you're distracting me. I can't do this!

And yet ... I could. I was still white-knuckling the wheel, fully tuned in to the road. But at the same time, I was engaged in communication with this presence. It was like my energy had split, and I was fully present in both experiences. A frequency of peace entered the car. Time stretched. The chaos around me didn't disappear, but it no longer held me hostage.

We spoke for thirty minutes, though it went by in the blink of an eye, with the conversation unfolding in layers I'd revisit again and again. Then, just as I approached my exit, the energy shifted. I dropped back into my body, moved into the right lane, and exited as if nothing had happened.

But everything had changed.

As soon as I got into the house, I scribbled down the messages I had received as fast as I could so as not to forget anything. It took up a whole page, but one line stood out to me:

"Are you ready, Brandi? Are you ready for what's coming?"

Those questions, and the information that followed, were a turning point, completely reframing this book, which was already in process, and my understanding of the work I am here to do.

That day didn't mark the beginning of my connection with this Source. It had been with me all along, moving through meditation, breathwork, dreams, and energy sessions. But this? This was different. This was direct. Immediate. Embodied.

It reminded me that we don't need to reach outside of ourselves to connect with wisdom. It already lives within us—quiet, steady, waiting for our attention. This book is a reflection of that inner resonance. You may call it Spirit, Source, Higher Self, Divine Intelligence, Universal Light ... or simply Knowing. You don't have to believe in anything. Just feel what's true for you.

If you're like most people, you have heard the term "spiritual journey" more times than you can count. You've also heard about "awakening," "ascension," and "enlightenment."

If you're wondering what they mean, I have been right there with you. I had no clue either, not until life delivered me some serious wake-up calls. I didn't seek out this path. In fact, I ran from it for decades. But eventually, the only thing left to do was surrender.

That's when the remembering began.

My path has been anything but linear, and I've played many roles, from a child beauty queen to a survivor of sexual and relationship trauma; a law enforcement officer and an addict; a patient and a healer; a skeptic of spirituality and a spiritual teacher, energy alchemist, and channeler of Divine wisdom.

I am still a wife and a mother, but a very different one than I used to be. It is only now, as I look back on those four decades spent in complete separation and forgetfulness of who I am, that I see this beautifully choreographed mosaic for my soul's growth. Each chapter, no matter how painful or confusing, led me closer to the truth of who I am—not the identity I had built, but the essence I had forgotten.

The same essence lives in you.

In the pages ahead, I will share the experiences that brought me to the brink of emotional and physical death, resulted in an actual ego death, and, ultimately, led to a deep unraveling and miraculous transformation. I'll share how messages came, not from some voice in the sky, but from a space of expanded consciousness that I tapped into when I stopped resisting and started listening. These teachings didn't arrive through books or doctrine, but through energy, frequency, and presence.

You may encounter terms such as awakening, embodiment, higher self, or frequency. Let them land how they will. The invitation is not to believe, but to feel, to allow something ancient and familiar within you to stir.

Whether you're already walking this path, just beginning, or still not sure you're ready, you're here for a reason. You've been guided. Let the energy of these pages meet you where you are and plant the seeds you're ready to hold. I ask only that you read with the eyes of a student, allowing seeds to be planted. If you are in a place of worry or fear or doubt, I will save you the suspense: this (life) is a big game, and I know how it ends. The Light wins.

Now, let's talk about what happens in between.

PART I

Before Awakening

There is a narrow way of living, one that feels normal because it is all that has been known. Like ants moving through the glass walls of an unseen container, most move through life focused on the next task, the next obligation, the next thing to fix. Wake up. Go to work. Pay the bills. Repeat.

This is the illusion of separation, the belief that life is happening to you, not through you. That you are at the mercy of circumstance. That control is survival, and surrender is weakness. Even those who sense a Divine plan often still feel powerless within it, unsure of their place in something so vast.

But there is more.

More than the ant farm.

More than the grind.

More than the stories you were taught to live inside.

The moment you begin to question the walls, a crack of light appears.

And through that opening, something begins to stir ...

SMILING FOR THE CAMERAS

The "ant farm" is built on systems, which is just another word for mechanisms on how life is "supposed" to work. These systems exist in every area of life—our families, school systems, medical care, and religious life. They can be different, depending on when and where we are born, but in every case, they are based on a structure created for us, not by us.

These systems, at one point or another, may have had a place and a purpose, BUT/AND, when we are locked into them, we cannot see ourselves clearly. We cannot see what people and experiences are meant to teach us.

Our families are our first and greatest teachers when it comes to boundaries. I have memories of being three years old—maybe even two and a half. Even if I didn't remember, there are plenty of pictures to remind me. I looked like a porcelain doll, with lipstick, blush, mascara; my hair was a cloud of perfect golden ringlets.

I remember the fashion shows—the catwalk stretching out before me, the lovely dresses and white ruffled underwear, the eyes of the audience. Then there were photoshoots when I was not clothed and very much wanted to be. The photo everyone wanted, the one that had them gushing, "She looks so cute!" had one tiny nipple exposed. It was the one that filled me with shame and embarrassment; it made me want to hide.

My parents had no awareness that I was being exploited or how I felt about it. All they knew was that they had this teacup beauty queen everyone cooed at and complimented and, by extension, complimented them. It never occurred to them that their three-year-old was being sold as a sex symbol.

I had a knowing that my true essence was love. The world was showing me something else. It was the world reflected to me each night when my mother put those foam curlers in my hair, and later, my younger sister's. We would cry because they were so painful and made it impossible to get comfortable on the pillow.

I was learning that I had to be pretty to be loved. I was learning to play the game.

It is clear to me now that this is when I split, when I unconsciously closed down my true self and began following the rules. They were as follows: when I got first place in a pageant, the adults around me were happy. I wanted everyone to be happy, so I learned to "perform." I unknowingly made myself responsible for how others were feeling, and put their feelings before my own.

For the next several years, I appeared in commercials, including one for Oscar Mayer wieners, print ads, and movies. My face was even on the Shrinky Dink box.

Everyone around me thought this was great; all the school I was missing, not a big deal. I, like many of us during childhood, was being trained to focus on the external and look outside myself for validation and love.

This was confirmed when, as I got older, Mom would say, "No one will love you if you're fat."

If you're thinking my childhood had a "Mommy Dearest" energy to it, you would be correct. But this is not a "hit piece" on my mother, though it might have been had I written this book ten years ago.

Mom said these things, not out of malice—in fact, she always clarified that *she* would always love me no matter what—but because at her level of awareness, this was what she knew to be true about the world.

It was the same unyielding stance she took on her own lovability. Growing up in a well-to-do Midwestern family in the 1950s, she had been taught that a woman's role was to look pretty and stay silent. If she did, she just might be lucky enough to get a man to love her.

Self-love was never even on the radar. She did meet a good man, my father, who loved and respected her for the rest of her life. She also had me and my younger sister, Buffy, who loved her as well. But without self-love, without the ability to fill herself up, she relied on us to do it for her. It was a role I would play for four decades, and there was never a day off.

Mom said other things as well, but those words, "No one will love you if you're fat," probably had the greatest effect. I internalized them; I unconsciously took on the belief that my external appearance was everything.

It was also very fragile; if I weren't diligent about maintaining my beauty, I would lose everything or, more likely, not have it in the first place. No surprise, then, that I became very self-conscious about my looks; no surprise that I later manifested dis-ease that caused me to lose that lovely blond hair.

On the other hand, added weight also would become my protector: "No one will love you if you're fat" became, "No one will prey on you, hurt you ..." and so on (more on that later).

Now, I look at photos from that time, when I was so ill I nearly died, and it is so clear: It was horrific, BUT/AND everything that made me beautiful was being released, stripped away, so I could find the real beauty within. It was all Divinely guided.

When we take on these dense beliefs, it is like heavy blankets weighing us down and dimming our light. The healing process is like lifting those blankets off, one by one. To learn to do this, I had to go back to my childhood, to connect with that little girl who never felt safe because no one ever taught her how.

I'm teaching her now.

You can try it with your own inner child. Put your hand on your heart, close your eyes. Slowly breathe in, breathe out. You will find them waiting there for you.

Remember, Mommy Dearest was once a wounded little girl too. It's about recognizing the cycle and breaking it.

THE TRAUMA BOX

You don't need a "special" spiritual awakening. We are getting opportunities all the time to awaken, as long as we are on this physical plane. Some are a subtle nudge; others feel like a storm destroying our lives; countless others fall somewhere in between. If we pass up one opportunity, we will be handed another … and another … and another, until we get the message.

The decision to take action (or not) on a growth opportunity is always ours. The question is, how do we *recognize* them as opportunities when they often have the appearance of ordinary life circumstances that we must fight through, endure, or heal from?

We do this by expanding our awareness to understand that there is much more going on than what we perceive with our five senses. Before awakening, I was given many "nudges" and many "storms," which I later came to understand as whispers from my Higher Self, calling me to this expanded awareness.

I recall being excited when my high school class was assigned *Siddhartha*, a novel based on the life of the Buddha. At the time, I was also drawn to crystals and wore them often. Looking back, I can see these things were speaking to a curiosity I had about spirituality.

Was reading *Siddhartha* an invitation to explore that further? Yes. However, I was also attending religious schools where we were taught about sins (i.e., premarital sex) and how we would be sent to hell for them. This judgment-based philosophy didn't feel good to me, and, since I didn't understand the difference between spirituality and religion at that age, I moved away from both.

This is one example of the subtle push and pull between what we are intuitively being called to and what the systems in the physical world are telling us. We are trained by everyone around us—our families, schools, the larger culture, the government, and so on—to see experiences through a certain lens. We label them positive and negative; we see the things we enjoy as "luck" and write off those we don't as "Good things don't happen to me," or "Money doesn't grow on trees," or whatever stories we tell ourselves.

How do we change this? By becoming curious, starting to unravel our experiences, and viewing them from an expanded perspective. It is trusting that we are always protected by, connected to, guided, and loved by the Divine, though it doesn't always feel that way.

There were several instances in my life when that protection was very obvious. Growing up, I was always pushing the limits to see what I could get away with. Was it typical childhood mischievousness, a reaction to past experiences, or simply a desire to expand past what I saw in my world? Probably all three.

We are all operating on several levels all the time. Before awakening, we are operating from the personality self and are aware only of what we're experiencing through the physical senses. We can't yet conceive of all that is happening to support us in the unseen realms.

Whatever the reason, I was certainly pushing the limits when my sixteen-year-old self cruised down Shea Boulevard in Phoenix one Friday at midnight. It was the late 1980s, the era of punk hairstyles and bands like Depeche Mode, Beastie Boys, and The Cure—"Love Song" or "No Sleep Till Brooklyn" might even have been blasting on the radio of my cute little red BMW.

Picture a scene from one of those great Brat Pack movies like *Sixteen Candles*, except I was nothing like Molly Ringwald. I was under the influence, not for the first time, as was the friend, a year younger, in the passenger seat beside me. I hadn't felt it when I got behind the wheel, but once we were on the road, it suddenly hit me … hard.

I was making a left onto Tatum Boulevard, a busy intersection, when the car sputtered and stalled. From there, everything happened in slow motion. My friend and I stared at each other; even if we had been sober, we would have had no clue what to do.

Then, out of nowhere, a police cruiser appeared, lights flashing. As the officer got out and slowly walked to the driver's side door, I was aware of feeling relieved and terrified at the same time.

"Do you need some help?" he asked.

With great effort, I forced myself to look at him and somehow managed to articulate what had happened and that yes, I definitely needed help. I felt how huge my eyes were; I was aware that I looked crazy. Surely, any minute the cop would notice, and I would be in deep trouble.

Instead, he turned around and walked back to his cruiser, then used it to gently push the BMW to the side of the road. We sat there, dazed, as he hooked jumper cables to the engines of the two cars and jumped the BMW's battery. Then, after wishing me a good night, he got in his car and left.

Did I feel gratitude? Sure, in that "Holy crap, I can't believe I got away with that" kind of way. That feeling, and the entire incident, was forgotten as soon as the BMW was fixed. I was, after all, a teenager.

I wouldn't know until decades later that this had been bigger than me not getting arrested and grounded by my parents. It wasn't even just about keeping my record clean so I could one day serve in law enforcement. It *was* all about Spirit intervening to keep me alive as I navigated this life journey, even when I was determined to self-destruct.

There were several other experiences, both before and after that night, with people who presented not as helpers but as predators. Sometimes, I avoided physical and emotional harm; other times, I didn't.

Every time, I was being guided and protected. Oftentimes, I dealt with these experiences and the emotions associated with them by putting them in "a box." I thought I was "moving on," but I was unknowingly holding that energy in my body.

Over the years, I would continue adding to that box every painful experience I endured; it contained every time I was not heard, and when I didn't hear myself.

Every traumatic event, whether it involves physical injury or not, carries an energy that remains in our body unless we move it.

During a stay at a Girl Scout camp, I had a knowing that I was unsafe. My memories are blurry, for which I am grateful, but I do recall waking up in a cabin other than my own.

When I asked the counselors about this, they didn't believe me, and I was dismissed. I knew I had to get out of there, but I wasn't sure how this was going to happen; the camp was out of town, and communication with parents was limited to one letter a week. "Coincidentally," I fell off a tire swing and hit my head, which gave me a reason to call home. The injury was not serious, but my mom and dad came to pick me up.

Years later, I had a driver's ed instructor who decided during a lesson that he had to stop at his home, which was at least ten miles from where we were supposed to be practicing, "to get something inside."

I remember sitting in his driveway, hearing him ask if I wanted to come in with him, and knowing that if I did, something awful would happen to me. At that moment, my cell phone (I had one of those early-model, enormous "brick" phones) rang. It was my dad. Whatever the driver's ed teacher was planning, that call made him think better of it. I got home safely and never told anyone about it because I felt stupid for driving out there and was afraid of getting in trouble. For years, I never thought about it again, but that experience was valuable for a few different reasons.

Let me explain. First, and perhaps most apparent, is that I was protected from this man. Second, even before the phone call interrupted his plan, I had a knowing that he did not have good intentions.

I was unconsciously feeling the difference between his energy and mine. I was sensing where I ended and he began. All of us are constantly encountering other energies and, whether they are healthy for us or not, they are always teaching us this.

Third, I had an opportunity to use my voice and tell the driver's ed teacher that no, I was not going to drive to his house. That feeling of being "stupid" for doing so was reminding me of that disconnect between my knowing and my action.

Of course, the closer a person is to us (i.e., family members, friends, partners), the harder it is to distinguish their energy from our own. My first love—I will call him "Scott"—is a good example of this.

Scott and I met when I was sixteen and he was seventeen. We were soon inseparable, and he became very close with my family as well. In fact, when his father kicked him out (he'd been expelled from his private school for speaking out against the school in the newspaper), my mom and dad let him live with us. They felt sorry for him; clearly, they thought he was a nice kid who had grown up in an unhealthy environment.

My parents had no idea that so much of what was happening between us was so inappropriate, and neither did I. He was my first love; this was my first consensual sexual experience; I had nothing to compare it to. After he graduated, Scott then moved to California to live with his mom, but we maintained a long-distance relationship.

Things imploded during a family vacation to San Diego right before my senior year of high school. I was really looking forward to it; a good friend of mine was coming along, plus I would get to see Scott. His mom's home was about forty-five minutes away from where we were staying, and when she heard about the trip, she invited us over for lunch.

It was all good … until I went into Scott's bedroom and found in his desk drawer a whole bunch of photographs of him having sex with other girls; in some, he had more than one partner. They looked to have been taken recently and certainly during the time we were together.

It was like a punch to the gut, and a layer of betrayal I had never felt before. There was no question about what I was going to do about it. I got my parents and my friend, and we drove back to the beach, where I put gifts Scott had given me, along with some of his personal belongings I'd brought from Arizona, out on the lawn.

It wasn't until about five years ago, when he was arrested and later convicted as a serial sex offender, that I fully realized the significance of that experience. Scott's victims were all teenage girls, the same age I was when we were together.

It also came out that he was a sex addict, something he had confessed to me years earlier, way before it was recognized as a real thing. This brought back all kinds of memories from the time we dated, now seen through a new lens. He had been grooming me, working out the patterns that would lead to his incarceration. If not for me "luckily" finding those photographs, who knows where it would have led?

This relationship was another challenge (aka invitation) to learn to love myself. And I accepted that invitation, *at the level of awareness I had at that time*. I broke up with him, but I also kept in touch with him and even hooked up with him several more times.

I was so wounded, and when we don't know how to move that energy, we keep going back for more. It also marked the beginning of a major spiral. My best friend of the last three years moved to Connecticut—another loss that absolutely devastated me. I did find a new friend group, and, ultimately, moved on from the breakup with Scott, but senior year of high school was really rough. Already a partier, I started smoking a lot more pot and could often be found in the parking lot with a joint between my lips. More importantly, I was still energetically carrying around the pain of those experiences.

The following year, I started college at the University of San Diego. In many ways, it was an extension of Xavier, my high school. Private, uppity, and Catholic—they were everything I was not. Still, going away to school was a chance to start over. I decided to pledge a sorority.

I was excited when I got to the mixer, held by the sorority I was pledging, and saw Carter, a boy I knew from home. A year older than me, he had gone to Brophy, the "brother" school to Xavier. We weren't what I would call close, but it was so nice to see a familiar face; I didn't know many people yet.

Carter seemed just as happy to see me. We hung out for the night; he called me his "little sister" and looked after me. I remember feeling so protected. When he asked me to go with him to get more beer, I didn't think anything of it; nor did I think anything of it when, instead of going to the store, he went to his apartment. At eighteen, I was still really naïve, so when my "big brother" said he had more beer in there, I went inside with him without a second thought.

That's when I heard, *Tell him you're on your period.*

It wasn't a voice outside me, of course, but like words flashing across my mind. It was the strangest thing, so random, untrue, and, in that moment, seemingly uncalled for.

It turned out Carter wasn't there for the beer. Before I knew it, and despite my clear NO, he was pushing me down and attempting to unbutton my pants. This could not be happening, only it was. That's when I heard it again.

Tell him you're on your period.

This time, I said the words. He got very angry, first punching the wall, then holding me down while he relieved himself on me. I know now that what he did was an assault; back then, I told myself I was lucky to be physically unharmed. I never thought about where the guidance that had saved me came from, nor did I realize how much the experience had affected me.

That energy went "in the box" and was shelved.

I quickly got acclimated to school, making friends and, like most college kids, going to local bars. Sometimes, I drank to the point that my judgment was clouded; sometimes, I met guys.

I was aware that they thought I was pretty, and that gave me a sense of confidence, even a sense of power. Most of those nights have faded to a blur of fun, music, and alcohol. Most of them, but not all.

His name was Ken, and he appeared to be like most guys I encountered: good-looking and cool to hang out with. We flirted at the bar, and I don't know who suggested what first, but we wound up going back to my house, which was empty at the time.

When we got there, something shifted, and I no longer wanted to be with him. I remember feeling a prick of fear and being unsure how to get out of it … and then … nothing.

When I woke the next morning, he was still there, and I had no memory of anything that had happened. Chalking it up to having had too much to drink, I got ready to drive him to work.

The ride was uneventful and quiet; then, as he got out of the car, Ken looked at me and said, "Daddy was a bad boy last night," as casually as if he had spilled something on the counter.

In that moment, everything came flooding back. How I had repeatedly said no; how I tried to stop him, but he was too strong. I remembered the terror and that awful feeling of being overpowered, of feeling like something to be preyed upon.

I felt very alone throughout this whole experience. At first, my roommate was very loving and supportive. She saw me come home that morning, realized something was very wrong, and listened to what had happened. She took me to the shower and wept with me.

After that, however, we never spoke about it again. It never occurred to me to report the sexual assault or tell my parents. All the things that commonly go through one's mind after something like this happens went through mine: I was drunk; I had taken Ken to my house, and so on, as if I were somehow culpable.

I did reach out to my good friend, who not only didn't believe me but went out with Ken the following week. After that, I buried it; I put that night and her betrayal in the box, where it would remain for decades.

At the same time, I beat myself up for the weight I gained and told myself it was "freshman fifteen." I changed colleges and told myself the new school was a better fit. What I thought was "moving on" was trapping energy that needed to move. It was collecting in all the muscles and cells of my body.

What I am about to say may be difficult to process, so let me preface it by saying I did not learn it from a book or a video, but rather through my experience communicating with Spirit, learning about energy, and figuring out how to move and alchemize it.

Sexual assault—or even the threat of it—is one of the most damaging things that can happen to a person while in a body, BUT/ AND, what I have come to understand is that Spirit does not see it the way we do.

Every event or exchange, whether perceived as positive or negative, whether it lasts for seconds or years, is an opportunity for growth. It is an opportunity to distinguish our energy from others and maintain our vibration, no matter what is happening around us. The predators were as much my teachers as the cop who helped me at that intersection.

When we're in the third dimension, which is just another way of saying that our current level of awareness is focused on the physical reality—what we can see, touch, and measure—we see things like child abuse, predators, and crime as isolated, often senseless, events.

In the fourth dimension, our perception begins to expand. We become aware that there's more going on beneath the surface—layers of collective trauma, broken systems, corruption, and hidden truths.

When we shift into the fifth dimension, we still see all of that, but we perceive it through the lens of spiritual growth. We begin to understand that even the most painful events can serve a higher purpose, offering our soul a chance to evolve. Ascension, in this context, simply means expanding your consciousness— elevating your perspective from fear, survival, and judgment to love, truth, and unity.

Each person chooses how to navigate life's challenges. Not everyone will choose the path of Light. Not everyone is meant to. And that's okay. There is no absolute right or wrong, only experience, growth, and remembering who we really are.

There is always a larger plan. Our souls are always safe. I can say this now, without equivocation, because of my experiences. The driver's ed teacher and the frat boy both presented me with opportunities to use my voice and trust the guidance I was being given.

All of these experiences, including the sexual assault, would be explained to me when I connected to Spirit. All of them presented me with an opportunity to learn to love myself unconditionally.

THE GREAT ESCAPE

While on the ant farm, with all its challenges over which we seem powerless, it is easy to want to escape. And when we cannot escape the circumstances that we feel have enslaved us, we try in various ways to escape the vessel we live in. We ply it with food and other substances; we give it to people who don't deserve it but are, unbeknownst to us, vibrating in the same frequency. In this way, we move away from the Light. We give away the means to move through anything: our power.

After the sexual assault, I ran as far as I could from myself, trying to regain the control I believed had been stolen from me. This manifested as twenty extra pounds, which were noticed and commented upon by my family when I went home for the holidays.

Their remarks about my clothes being tight or that perhaps I had been enjoying the food at school a little too much only made me feel more isolated. Nobody ever asked me if there was some emotional reason behind the weight gain. In their defense, they didn't know to ask, and I certainly did not volunteer information.

I did confide in a couple of friends from high school about the sorority mixer and the sexual assault that followed. It turns out that high school popularity is a powerful currency even after graduation. My friends didn't believe me. They did, however, stay friends with him, and some remain so to this day. It was all very isolating and compounded the lack of support I'd gotten from my friend at USD when I told her about the sexual assault.

Then, something incredible happened. I met a guy (I will call him Trevor to protect his privacy) and quickly fell for him. After spending the spring semester going back and forth between San Diego and Phoenix, I moved home and transferred to Arizona State University so we could be together. Looking back, I was also unconsciously trying to distance myself from the assault.

> *Again, we are operating on several levels. External events, good as well as bad, in our physical environment can distract us from what's going on inside. When we turn inward and get to know ourselves without these distractions, we can discern what's happening energetically and clean it up. Every experience, including blessings, is then elevated and welcomed with more joy and light.*

Trevor was every bit as great as he appeared when we first met—kind, gentle, and respectful. We were happy, and when, after three years of dating, he asked me to marry him, I accepted without reservation. My life felt like it was falling into place ... which is why what happened was so confusing.

Two years later, and with the wedding imminent and paid for, I called it off. He was devastated, and I was devastated at having hurt him. I also had no idea why I was doing this; I was still in love with him and attracted to him. He was still kind and gave every indication that he would make a great husband. We were in a long-distance relationship at that point, which might have allowed me to talk myself out of marrying him, but, bottom line, I just knew I shouldn't marry him.

Like I said earlier, I've played all parts—"victim" and "villain." Years later, I contacted Trevor, apologized, and really shared from my heart where I was when I called off the wedding.

It all worked out—he has a wife and two daughters—but at the time, it was very traumatic. Also, I had been carrying around that regret, one of the biggest in my life, since then. Forgiving myself and reaching out to him was healing for both of us.

Sometimes we have a knowing without knowing why. We can choose to be frustrated and second-guess ourselves, or we can choose to trust. Sometimes, this means someone else gets hurt. No matter how difficult this is, our first priority must always be to honor ourselves. To do anything else dishonors everyone.

At the time, I didn't know any of this; I just felt awful. Who did I think I was, throwing away a great guy like that? To convince myself I had made the right decision, I soon got involved with someone else. Not surprisingly, considering how I was feeling, that relationship was a very different one.

I was twenty-three and working in loss prevention, a role I had been in for years and really enjoyed. My new boyfriend was my boss, and at first, I looked up to him. He was also an abuser, and though he never touched me except to grab me by the wrist, he spent every moment controlling me.

We had pagers at the time, and I had to page him with certain codes at certain times to let him know where I was and with whom. He even knew, to the second, how long it took me to get to his apartment, which I had moved into. It was horrible, and what I felt I deserved after what I had done to Trevor.

A daily drinker, he thought nothing about getting behind the wheel drunk. Every day after work, he stopped to get a twelve-pack of beer. Sometimes, he passed out in his truck with its motor running, a lit cigarette in his hand. Yet, he still always had the time to have a chokehold on my life. I sometimes prayed he would get a DUI or even get in an accident, just so I could get some peace, not to mention prevent him from hurting someone else.

In the end, he wound up breaking up with me. Not only that, he did it because I was experimenting with substances, which he decided was worse than his drinking. He shamed me for this and looked down on me like I was trash. He was reflecting exactly how I felt about myself. In my brokenness, I begged and begged him to take me back, apologizing and promising to change. I no longer knew who I was.

> *We don't get our power back by fixing other people or changing our circumstances. True power comes from within. We reclaim it by reconnecting with our body, choosing thoughts and practices that lift our energy, and learning to hold that higher state, even when the world around us feels chaotic.*

After being released from this situation, I spent the next few years turning things around—living with friends, becoming a manager at work, and finishing school. There was fun too; I had a big personality, and I loved going out and connecting with others.

With men, I adopted the role of aggressor, adopting an "I'll hurt them before they hurt me again" kind of mindset. No one who met me during this time would have guessed that I was carrying around years of unprocessed trauma. They only saw the party girl, the one who was up for anything.

My continued experimentation with substances perpetuated this image and provided me with a welcome distraction, an escape from the body that had attracted abusers. To my delight, it also had another side effect: weight loss.

Suddenly, I was thin, something I equated with attractiveness and therefore worthiness. This was confirmed by the positive feedback I received whenever I saw my family and friends. How I did it was of far less concern; I even recall my grandmother mentioning a diet pill called "Black Beauties," considered the magic bullet in her day.

I'm not sure when I crossed that subtle line between partying and addiction, or when I realized I was damaging my body. However, I do remember mentioning to my mom that I wanted to clean up my act. Her response: Could I do this and stay skinny? I knew then that I didn't see a way out.

"No one will love you if you're fat, Brandi."

I no longer had to hear my mother's voice in my head; the words had become so woven into my self-perception that they felt like my own.

Ultimately, it was Dennis, whom I met shortly after that conversation, who showed me a way out, or at least facilitated it. Our first encounter had all the makings of a meet-cute in a movie. I was buying sunglasses in AZP, a shop that sold skateboards, snowboards, and other adventure gear, when I saw him. A six-foot-three "skater dude," he would have been hard to miss. I thought he was *hot*. During our brief meeting, I learned that AZP was his store.

Shortly after that, I bumped into him again while out with friends at Anderson's Fifth Estate, a bar in Scottsdale. Seizing the moment, I walked up to him, handed him my number, and said, "You should call me sometime."

He didn't wait long, maybe a couple of days, before asking me out for dinner. It was to be my first "real" date … and my last.

That night, over sushi and sake, I had the awareness of a feeling I had never experienced before. It was at once so subtle and so strong that I told my mother the next day that I was going to marry him. I made the same announcement to Dennis shortly after that.

It was the feeling of home.

It bears repeating: if we don't follow our knowing, if we don't follow the breadcrumbs because we don't have all the answers or can't see where it leads or we want to avoid disappointing someone else, we are not only subverting the plan Spirit and our Higher Self has for us, we are also interfering with the paths of those around us.

Three months later (after I dared him to marry me), we eloped … something that would not have happened if I had gone through with the wedding to Trevor two years earlier.

During those three months of dating, that feeling of home was reaffirmed time and time again. As we lay in bed at night, Dennis would talk to me about star systems, planets, and galaxies, and how they all worked. I had always been interested in those things, but this connection went beyond the cerebral. It felt like magic.

He also revealed a strength he would display throughout our marriage. When he realized the lengths I would go to in order to play the perfect daughter, an ultimatum swiftly followed: I leave the people-pleasing child behind and step into being a healthy adult who thinks for herself.

Dennis was by my side when I went to my parents' house and informed them that I was choosing a healthy lifestyle. He also supported me in my recovery endeavors.

I had also found someone who brought incredible support to my life. And, over the years, he would become my very backbone.

This was incredible, BUT/AND it was also setting up a dynamic, unconsciously created and consented to by both of us, that was perpetuating my sense of disempowerment and, ultimately, would have to be dismantled for me to heal.

We can only meet people in the frequency we're holding and at our level of awareness at the time.

CONFESSIONS OF A
"KNOW-IT-ALL" ATHEIST

We don't become intuitive because we are special or more evolved than another. Spirit doesn't play favorites or grant powers to those who sing for their supper. Christian, Muslim, or Jew, Buddhist or Hindu, agnostic or atheist, we are all hardwired to tap into universal or cosmic knowledge.

For most of my life, I believed in nothing but the ant farm, yet I just knew things I "couldn't" have known. I also, despite my lack of awareness, understanding, or energy, often acted on those knowings; I simply credited them to Brandi, my human self.

I have since learned, through my recollections or in communication with my Higher Self, angels, and Spirit, that each time I was either being guided *toward* some person or action I needed to take, or *away* from some kind of harm. This was evidenced by several decisions, unexplainable to me, in my personal life; however, it extended to my professional life as well.

As mentioned earlier, my career began in loss prevention while I was still in college. I worked at some of the largest department stores—Macy's, Saks, and Robinson's May. I was really good at it, so good that I was consistently the highest monthly producer. I just always seemed to know who was going to steal.

The biggest case I worked on involved another manager, who was stealing St. John's business suits and hiding them *in the ceiling of her office*. Today, I laugh and think, *Ummm … hello, Brandi, nobody is that good unless they have some serious spiritual support*, but back then, it didn't even enter my mind. My ego was running the show; my "religion" was science and logic.

Let's be clear: I am not bashing my ego. In fact, I am grateful for the ways it protected me and pushed me to survive and thrive. It gave me the confidence to excel in my work and the perseverance to get through the challenges of college and graduate school.

> *The ego is not negative; it is just another aspect of us, one that helps us navigate the physical world. The problem (lack of alignment) arises when we are listening solely to the ego and ignoring the whispers from our higher self, our guides, and Spirit.*

After graduating, I transitioned from loss prevention to law enforcement, a move that felt natural and exciting to me. Initially, I was interested in becoming a police officer, but I chose to pursue a career in probation instead because it was more academically challenging. More education, better pay, I figured.

Much of my job involved writing and presenting reports for the court, but I also supervised gang members under community supervision in central Phoenix, and I found I loved both them and the work. I went back to school for my Master's in Education Leadership, thinking I would eventually teach criminology.

After a few years in probation, I learned of a new, specialized domestic violence unit being formed in Maricopa County. It was the 1990s, abusers were finally starting to be held more accountable, and this new unit was partnering with local law enforcement to deal with felony offenders. It was also the first armed unit of its kind in the county. Though I enjoyed what I was doing, this was an opportunity I couldn't pass up.

I loved everything about being part of this unit. After the warrant officers, we were the first unit in the department to be armed and got to train at the Phoenix Police Training Academy, which was really cool.

I loved carrying a gun; I loved my boss, who was very supportive, and Kristi, my partner and best friend. I loved working with victims, with whom half my time was spent.

I felt like I belonged, that I was needed and making a difference, that I was living my purpose. I had every intention of continuing to move up the career ladder. Things were also going well on the home front; Dennis and I were happy together and had welcomed our first child, Dennis III, into the world.

Now, if someone had told me that this job was another way of getting external validation and masking my lack of self-love, I would have a) told them I didn't understand a word of what they just said, and b) politely suggested they sell crazy somewhere else.

The work I was doing was of great value to people in need, and I truly believed I was doing what I was meant to do. BUT/AND, there were other things happening on an energetic level that I was not aware of.

It is no coincidence that during this time I was the heaviest of my life. Every day, Kristi and I saw awful things that humans do to each other, to their kids, their pets, and themselves. And, like so many in law enforcement and the armed forces, we made jokes to deflect.

In doing so, we were bypassing the heart rather than processing our feelings. We were completely unaware of this, of course, as well as what we were taking on energetically.

Back then, my definitions of energy included what your body needs for a workout and what a lamp needs to illuminate a room. I certainly didn't know how to discern energy that wasn't mine and move it out of my body. I now know that those added pounds were my body going into protection mode.

We are energetic beings, absorbing everything around us, all the time. This goes beyond things that involve us directly to include world events and things we witness happening to others. Those emotions, that energy, also need to be processed and transmuted.

At the same time, I was receiving guidance and protection that often showed up as "knowings." Whenever this happened, I looked for the logical reason for the information I received or chalked it up to "coincidence," even when that information saved my life.

When I was pregnant with my second child, I went into labor early, at thirty-two weeks. They kept me in the hospital until week thirty-five, when, thankfully, I gave birth to another healthy son, Billy.

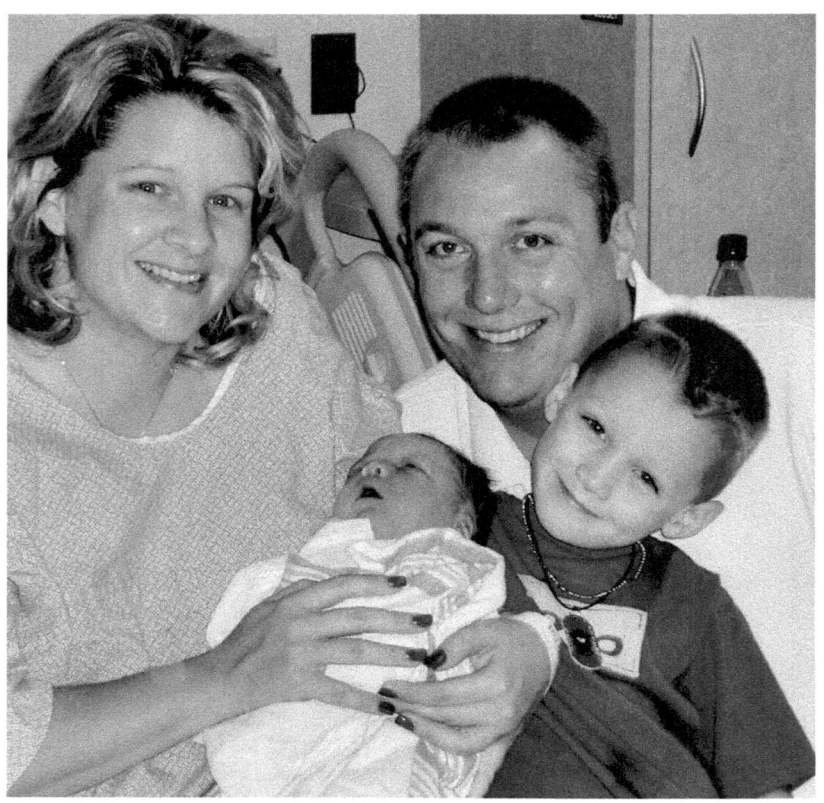

From there, things went according to plan. I took my maternity leave; Kristi took on my caseload. I had every intention of going back in six weeks, just as I had when Dennis was born. I had Billy's daycare picked out and every detail planned. I was looking forward to getting back into the swing of things.

It happened on the Friday before I was supposed to return to work. Out of nowhere, I suddenly got a strong feeling not to go in on that Monday. I dismissed this as "hormonal"; after all, plenty of new moms were reluctant to leave their babies.

Sure, my husband and I had briefly talked about my staying home, but that was theoretical at this point. I had been waiting to go back, I had prepared, and yet the feeling wouldn't go away. By Friday evening, I found myself typing out an email to my boss requesting a two-week extension.

On Sunday night, I received an email that my extension had been granted. When I reached out to Kristi to let her know, she mentioned that Darnell Clements was coming into the office on Monday. I knew Darnell well; he was a repeat domestic violence offender, and his wife and four kids, including two-year-old twins, were his victims.

Apparently, he had violated probation and would be arrested when he got to the office. This is where we made most arrests because the Scottsdale Police Department, which we worked closely with, didn't transport offenders. We would give the offender an excuse for why we needed them to come in, then we'd call Scottdale PD and let them know; they would position themselves at the exits. The way the office was set up, the officers could see inside as they approached from the back door.

That Monday, they went through the usual protocol. Clarence was directed to see me, and Kristi called the PD. Things took a horrible turn when he figured out that he was going to be arrested and, per the terms of his court sentence, sent back to prison.

He removed a gun from his waistband and, as he was lifting it to aim at Kristi, the Scottsdale police were coming down the hallway. They saw him just in time and fired, killing him. Clarence hit the desk and fell on the floor, leaving a puddle of blood there. I had seen a lot throughout my career, but seeing that dark stain on the carpet when I went in to retrieve my personal belongings and pack up my desk was truly jarring.

Had I been there, had I ignored that feeling, I would have been standing across from him when it happened. I wouldn't have been on my game, having been out of the office for weeks, and I wouldn't have been armed. During my pregnancy, I'd been unable to go to the firing range, something we were required to do quarterly to requalify for having a firearm. Because of this, I had to surrender my weapon.

When I heard the news, I knew I would tender my resignation and surrender my dream of serving in law enforcement. Though I didn't believe in anything spiritual, I did have the sense of being spared; the reason, I assumed, was so I could be home, taking care of my children.

Spirit and our Higher Self are always talking to every one of us. Our work is to feel our emotions and clear the energy from our bodies so we can hear them.

FISHING HOOKS

We always have complete sovereignty over our energy and where we invest it.

After expansion, we get to a certain space where we can hold our frequency and maintain our energy without sacrificing ourselves. This does not happen overnight. It's a muscle and, like any muscle, we have to build it up. We do this by starting to notice where we are giving our energy. We start to see what's not filling us up, which is just another way of saying it doesn't feel good.

Imagine our energy as fishing hooks that we cast out into the world. We cast it toward people and situations in our lives; we cast it toward medical and educational systems when we believe they are the ultimate authority, and we cast it toward the news media when we buy into their stories.

Before awareness, it seems like these people, situations, and systems have their hooks in us, and we are at their mercy. The truth is that we can reel those hooks back in any time we want. We just don't realize it, and this is how we give away our power—hour after hour, day after day, year after year. We allow circumstances to shape us, rather than the other way around, whether we are talking about our health, finances, relationships, or world events.

This gets especially tricky when we're talking about being of service to others. Justice has always been a motivator for me. It is part of who I am in this lifetime; it is what drew me to law enforcement.

It has also been an energetic "tripwire" of sorts. When I saw a situation I perceived as unfair to someone, it angered and frustrated me. I felt a pull to make it right, to the point that I would take on the energy of that situation on another's behalf.

Eventually, I came to realize, as you will, that if I were overinvesting in one situation or person, I would have nothing to give to someone else who really needed it.

Then, the question was no longer whether or not to give to or help someone or something. Takers are going to take. It was, "If I am overgiving to the point that I am depleting myself, what am I accomplishing? How am I being of service then?"

As you learn to manage and maintain your energy, you will inevitably disappoint people. If it comes down to disappointing someone else or yourself, always choose someone else.

This is an uncomfortable truth to accept, especially for caretakers and advocates. They are working so hard to fix things that they don't recognize their efforts to control outcomes. They don't see how, when they are not showing themselves the love they are giving to others, they are feeding the ego self, not the soul.

How do I know this? Because I had to learn it for myself ... the hard way.

Aside from my mother, my younger son, Billy, has been my greatest teacher with regard to where I was casting my energetic fishing hooks. In fact, they were teaching me some of the same lessons about enmeshment and codependency. I didn't learn it as a daughter, so I was given another chance to do so as a mother.

Like all parents, I wanted more than anything for my kids to feel safe and carefree—to be children for as long as possible. I also wanted their childhoods to be what mine wasn't, meaning I wanted to instill in them the belief that anything was possible, that they were beautiful and deserving of love, no matter what they looked like on the outside.

Like most parents, when my kids were doing well, I took it as validation of my excellent mothering skills. My experience with my first child backed this up. Dennis was an easy baby and taught himself to read at three. People regularly complimented my husband and me on what a terrific job we were doing.

Billy would completely disrupt this illusion. From a young age, his natural active state was one of hyperawareness, hypervigilance, and, to some degree, anxiety.

Every child is a sovereign soul who comes into this world with their own plans and roles to play in the lives of those around them, both as teachers and students. Whereas Dennis showed me how to love and believe in myself, Billy was more of a teacher, pushing my limits and challenging me to look at things—and myself—from a different, deeper perspective. His plans and lessons were also affected by what was going on in his environment.

The day of the shooting, my whole world changed. It wasn't the first time a defendant under my supervision had died; in fact, several had killed themselves, including two at the jail immediately after I arrested them.

This time was different. My body, which was still recovering from the early labor and hospitalization, went into a state of fight or flight. I was frozen with fear, but I didn't even realize it.

Of course, the what-ifs did come in. What if I had been in the office? What if I wasn't so "lucky" (because that's how I saw it) the next time? But I wasn't present enough to fully process the experience, and, as I had done so often in the past, I negated my feelings and pushed them down.

I believed I had to leave law enforcement and become something I never wanted to be: a stay-at-home mom.

That's the thing with fear: it tricks us into thinking we have
no choices.

As I had suspected it would, giving up my career sucked. I was used to getting up and out of the house each morning, contributing to society in a way unique to law enforcement and other first responders.

The business of helping others is hard to beat, especially when you're getting accolades for it, as I was. It made me feel good about myself. Plus, I genuinely loved it. It was what had cured me of post-partum depression after my first son was born.

Now I felt like I had been stripped of part of what made me, *me,* and I resented it. I also hated leaving Kristi. We were a great team, and every day had been an adventure. We had planned to move up together, and I felt like I had let her down.

I want to be clear: there is nothing wrong with taking pride in your work and enjoying the recognition you get for it. However, when it's the source of your self-worth and/or you are not connected with your heart space while doing it, it takes its toll on you physically and mentally.

In reality, I had not lost myself by giving up my job. I believed
I had lost myself because I gave away my power to a situation.

I fell into a deep depression, never imagining how this might affect the infant in my care twenty-four-seven. Looking back, I can see how Billy's hypervigilance, that sense of always being "on guard," definitely has something to do with the first months of his life.

This is not about blaming myself, though I certainly did my fair share of that over the years, but about recognizing the level of awareness I had at the time. I had no idea what it meant to "project" onto another person, that his nervous system would absorb, and be affected by, my vibration.

At some point, I decided that if I was going to be a stay-at-home mom, I would be the best stay-at-home mom ever. I dove in and devoted myself to my kids with the same level of commitment and attention to detail as I had in my career. Dennis continued to thrive, seemingly without any help from me or my husband. He made parenting look so easy, and I judged myself as a mom based on him.

When Billy began to struggle, I did the same, this time asking, "What kind of mom does that make me?" I was, unknowingly, of course, repeating a couple of patterns here. First, I was seeing my son as a reflection of myself, which was what my mother had done when I was in those beauty pageants as a kid. Second, I was getting my self-worth from my performance as a parent, just as I had gotten it from my performance as a law enforcement officer. Third, I was giving my power away to systems, in this case, the educational system, by trying to fit into a box—that being the school's expectations of what exemplary parents were supposed to be like.

I was being presented with opportunities to shift these patterns … and they would be presented again and again until I caught on.

Both my sons attended the same small K-8 school, with the same teachers and the same teams that had been in place for a long time.

Everyone adored Dennis, who was smart and easy to get along with and went on to be the student class president. The school became another thing to love about our small community; the teachers became my friends.

I had an expectation that they would show up in the same way for Billy. But Billy didn't fit in any of the boxes; a wise and sensitive soul, he knew what people were thinking and feeling. He also learned differently from other kids.

I was hurt and hardened when I witnessed those teachers treat him with complete unfairness and none of the affection they'd shown his brother. The reality was that they lacked the proper resources, training, time, and support to do so, but rather than acknowledging the broken system, they blamed the student. I didn't think of it in those terms back then. All I saw was the injustice, and that sent me into overdrive.

Advocating for Billy became my full-time job. I didn't just join the PTSA, I became its president; this way, I could be on campus and connected with the school administrators.

When I wasn't communicating with teachers and advocates, I was taking Billy to doctors' appointments and to get treatments and therapies. We tried various meds as well. My husband and I did everything Western medicine told us to do, but Billy still struggled to show up the way the teachers wanted him to.

It was an honor to be my son's advocate, BUT/AND I had no idea what this was doing to my body: a) I didn't know how energy worked, so I couldn't maintain my own energy, and b) as is often the case with parents, I was absorbing everything Billy was going through as if it were happening to me. This was in addition to decades of trauma I was already holding in my body.

At the same time, I was also being given another crash course in the systems that largely govern the physical world. It doesn't matter if it is law enforcement, education, medicine, or media; these systems are both energetic traps and opportunities to liberate ourselves from illusion. The illusion is that these systems have the ultimate authority over our soul's path; breaking free means becoming aware of the illusion and taking inspired action that opens a new timeline (path) for us.

What do I mean by "inspired action"? It can be anything from noticing a disempowering story we are telling ourselves and changing it, to asking Spirit/higher self/angels for help, setting boundaries with our partner, seeking another medical opinion, and so on.

Inspired action can be reflecting on how we have been showing up in a certain situation, or life in general, and making a different choice moving forward.

Billy truly was a mirror for me, and, as is so often the case, that mirror was hard to look at. I too had acted out in school—in kindergarten, I was sent to the principal's office for chasing the boys on the playground. In sixth grade, I was suspended for opening ketchup packets and putting them on a teacher's chair. I was "a lot," but no one ever suggested I might have ADHD, possibly because it was much more common in boys.

As mentioned earlier, the academic piece was also challenging for me, but I could never figure out why. Everyone at the private high school I attended seemed so much smarter than I was. Looking back, that wasn't the case at all; I just learned differently.

In college, I went through five universities and five majors. Eventually, I figured out how to make it work so well that I went on to get my master's, but it felt like an uphill battle the whole way.

Distractedness, executive function delays, and procrastination were constant issues, and I recall many times when I waited to write papers for my master's degree, as well as reports for work, the night before they were due.

When I was recovering from addiction, I was diagnosed with severe depression and put on antidepressants, but again, there was no inquiry or discussion about the possibility of ADHD symptoms. Prozac was supposed to fix everything. This was the start of a twenty-plus-year consumption of mood-altering pharmaceuticals.

It wasn't until Billy's diagnosis that I truly began to wonder if I had some of the same stuff going on. Several more years would pass before I was subjected to a full psychological evaluation (more on that later) and diagnosed with ADHD.

That full-circle moment would bring the realization that, in part, I had been protecting Billy because, unconsciously, I was trying to protect myself. In advocating for him, I was learning to advocate for myself. I was learning to use my voice for the first time. I was also learning a great deal about compassion and empathy.

This was all part of the Divine plan orchestrated by my Higher Self.

My body had already been through decades of trauma, and taking on Billy's stuff as my own would put me over the edge. I was moving toward the biggest crash and the biggest lesson of my life—the breakdown that would lead to the breakthrough.

UNEXPECTED GIFT

Surrender is not giving up or giving in, as we typically understand it. Surrender is releasing control, pulling our energy back from a situation, and stepping into faith that all will unfold according to the Divine plan, in Divine timing.

I am alive today because I surrendered, because I stopped fighting against or trying to control a systemic illness that seemed to have no name and no solution, but was draining my life force energy.

Long before that, however, I had another opportunity to learn the significance of surrender and how it operates energetically in our lives. This experience was also a testament to the fact that a soul's plan (in this case, the soul of my son Billy) to come here will not be thwarted, not even by the laws of science.

In other words, Billy was teaching me even before he was conceived.

My first pregnancy happened easily, thanks to a round of antibiotics that canceled out the birth control pills I was taking at the time. I even know it happened on the Fourth of July—just one of those cute, "happy surprise" stories we can sometimes take for granted.

Given this, when my husband and I decided a couple of years later to have a second child, we never imagined it would be so difficult. After several months of trying, I went to a reproductive endocrinologist, which these days is a common step for couples having trouble conceiving.

Back then, it was less popular, though my doctor, Dr. Drew Moffitt, was already known as "the guy" in the Phoenix area for women dealing with infertility and/or high-risk pregnancies, especially those carrying multiple babies.

Since I conceived so easily the first time, I was classified as having "secondary infertility," which has a higher success rate of overcoming because the underlying causes are easier to determine than "primary infertility."

A routine surgical procedure, where they go in and basically "Roto-rooter" your fallopian tubes, seemed promising. When that didn't work for me, I had further testing and was diagnosed with polycystic ovary syndrome (PCOS). This is a hormonal imbalance that causes a host of symptoms from irregular periods and weight gain to insulin resistance, skin issues, and the inability to ovulate on your own.

In my case, there were a dozen or so eggs in my ovaries, but due to the hormonal imbalance, they weren't releasing. The treatment for this is injections that stimulate the release.

Infertility is an emotional roller coaster, and not just because they are pumping you full of hormones—that would have been bad enough. It's the hoping and dreaming for that child that builds with each treatment, only to be crushed when it doesn't work. We did several unsuccessful cycles of the hormone injections, followed by cycles of insemination.

On one of those cycles, I got pregnant. After a couple of years of trying, we were thrilled and beyond relieved.

It's so easy to forget about the roller coaster.

A week or two later, my first ultrasound revealed that the pregnancy was ectopic, meaning the embryo hadn't made it all the way into the womb but had implanted in the fallopian tube.

I was completely and utterly devastated; in fact, at this point in my life, it was the worst thing I had ever experienced. In addition to the sorrow and loss of expectations, I felt a tremendous responsibility to give my son a sibling.

What I wasn't as consciously aware of was the story I was telling myself about the weight I'd gained with my first pregnancy. In my head, I was connecting the weight gain with my inability to get pregnant again, and I was shaming myself about it.

Never underestimate the power of our thoughts and our energy to affect the physical—our bodies, our environment, and those around us.

The other reality I faced when I heard the news that day was the risk to my health. Ectopic pregnancies are not viable, but the fetus is still growing, and without medical intervention, it will cause the fallopian tube to rupture. If this happens, you can bleed internally; in fact, in countries without available medical treatment, it is a leading cause of maternal death during the first trimester.[1]

Some women with ectopic pregnancies get surgery; in my case, they opted to give me a shot of methotrexate, a drug often used to treat cancer. It stops the embryo's heart, which broke my heart all over again. Then you wait for your body to release it, like a miscarriage, and have a normal flow.

That is not what happened to me. Instead, I was about to have my first brush with death.

This was a Friday, and the following day we were supposed to join another family in Rocky Point, a Mexican town just sixty miles south of the Arizona border. It was our son's spring break, and Dennis and I had taken the week off work, which was a really big deal for us.

---

[1] O.L. Lawani, O.B. Anozie, & P.O. Ezeonu, (2013). Ectopic pregnancy: a life-threatening gynecological emergency. *International journal of women's health*, 5, 515–521. https://doi.org/10.2147/IJWH.S49672

When we told the doctors about the trip, they said it was out of the question because I could rupture at any time. Now I was devastated not only because I couldn't carry the baby to term, but because my son wouldn't get to go on the vacation we had been so looking forward to.

The following Monday, I decided to take him to As You Wish, one of those places where you paint your own pottery. If we couldn't go away, at least we could spend our week off doing fun things together.

We were sitting at the table painting when I realized something was wrong. I didn't know what it was exactly, but I suddenly felt cold and dizzy and kind of spacy, like I wasn't thinking clearly. Then I started feeling nauseous.

From there, everything seemed to move in slow motion. I called my husband at work, and although I don't recall exactly what I said, I remember speaking in a casual tone; I didn't want to alarm him or my son.

Then I called my mom, told her what was happening, and asked her to meet me at my house to take care of him. She immediately got in her car and drove over from my parents' home in the West Valley.

Thankfully, we only lived a few miles away from As You Wish; still, I truly don't know how I drove. As it was, I barely made it in the door and onto the bed in the guest room off the garage. Within minutes, my mom and Dennis, who had left work right after I called him, showed up at the same time.

A call to the doctor's office confirmed what we already knew: I had to get to the hospital immediately. It was quite a long drive, and I was in and out of consciousness the whole time. When we got there, there was no preamble, just a rush to prep me for emergency surgery.

I had indeed ruptured and was bleeding internally. They caught it just in time.

It was the strangest thing. I could feel everyone else's fear and could sense the urgency; I also knew I was dying. Yet, I didn't feel fear like the ego self normally would. It was more of an understanding of what was happening on some deeper level, but without the panic.

I can remember seeing the operating room lights above me.

Later, I knew I was lucky to wake up and that I had come back for a reason.

I thought of that trip to Mexico and how, despite the doctor's warning, the decision to go or not had been a toss-up. I remembered thinking I had already taken the methotrexate shot, and women have miscarriages all the time. The risk didn't seem to warrant disappointing the others.

That day ended my dream of adding to our family. I had lost the ruptured fallopian tube on one side and didn't know the viability of my remaining ovary. It was unlikely, the doctors said, that I would get pregnant without more invasive treatments.

The finality of it was crushing, but the experience of nearly dying shifted my perspective. My son had almost lost me, but he didn't, and I was incredibly grateful for this, for the opportunity to be able to continue mothering him.

What right did I have to pursue these treatments and not be grateful for what I already had? And, truly, I had so much—a great family, a nice home, and a career I loved.

This gratitude allowed me to move through the experience. I don't know that I actually healed—more likely, I put it in a box and put the box on a shelf, as I had done with other painful events in my life.

But I walked away from that dream, walked away from that goal. I gave away everything I had been holding onto—the cribs, the clothes, and the toys—for the last five years in the hopes of having another baby.

And I walked away from that pain.

I surrendered and, one year later, I got pregnant with Billy.

To recap: I had one fallopian tube left, which in some cases reduces the chances of becoming pregnant. A much larger issue was that I had not ovulated on my own in years. How did this happen?

Since I'd had an ectopic pregnancy before, they got me in for a scan as soon as I told them I thought I was pregnant. On the scan, they could see a corpus luteum cyst, which is essentially a fluid-filled structure that develops after the egg is released, on my ovary.

They could also tell that my fallopian tube on one side *reached over* with those finger-like things to grab the egg from the other side.

That's what was happening on the physical. Energetically, it was the surrender that allowed me to get pregnant again.

I had stopped fighting against it; I had released resistance. Though I didn't think about it in those terms at the time, I was going into flow with what the Universe wanted for me. Once I was in flow, I then had the space to conceive without any medical intervention.

PART II

Breakdown To Breakthrough

There is a moment, silent and invisible to the world, when everything begins to slip.

You don't know it yet, but the life you've built is unraveling.

Not from failure, but from truth.

You're still fighting.

Holding on to routines that no longer feel good, to stories that no longer fit, to a version of yourself you no longer recognize.

Your body is breaking.

Your spirit is tired.

But you keep pushing, because that's all you know.

There's a stirring in your chest you can't explain.

A sense that something is wrong, but no words to name it.

You go through the motions, perform the roles, and smile when needed, all while quietly wondering how much longer you can hold it all together.

It feels like survival.

Like you're losing pieces of yourself, one thought, one symptom, one silent breakdown at a time.

And yet, you try harder.

Because letting go feels like giving up.

Because you don't yet know that what's falling apart is what was never meant to stay.

This is the in-between.

The sacred pause before everything changes.

Not yet surrendered.

Not yet softened.

Just … breaking.

Slowly.

Quietly.

Divinely.

THE YEAR THAT CHANGED EVERYTHING

The year 2014 was the start of the seismic shift in my awareness, which is to say that my life as I knew it really began to crumble. Energetically, this process had begun in 2012, a time when a lot of awakenings happened, and a lot of people came "online." For me, it took a bit longer; things weren't bad enough yet.

That would come later.

Certainly, 2012 was rich in opportunities for awakening. While driving with my family through Southern California, I noticed huge billboard signs along the highway advertising lap band surgery. Of course, I'd heard of these procedures, but I never really considered getting one.

Now, after a trip to the beach where I had felt uncomfortable in a bathing suit, these signs with their "after" pictures of perfect bodies put a bug in my head. My husband was opposed to the idea, but I had made up my mind.

What followed was a nightmare that would last for years. Not only was I in constant pain and discomfort after the procedure, but everything I ate came back up. I couldn't control the vomiting, which sometimes happened a dozen times a day.

I did, however, become an expert at hiding it, often by "wiping my mouth" with a napkin in the middle of a dinner conversation. No one was the wiser, and I continued to suffer in silence. What I *wasn't* doing was losing weight. Something was definitely wrong.

I had to have five separate "revision" surgeries, where they went in and repositioned the band, but it only got worse. Eventually, the doctors figured out that my stomach had prolapsed, or flipped over, and I had to have an emergency surgery. This was yet another time I was brought back from the brink of death.

Now, back to 2014 …

It all started early in the year when my mother got into a serious car accident, breaking everything from the hips down. She had to spend time in rehab, and when she got out, she decided to have a gastric sleeve so she could lose the weight she had gained while unable to move post-accident.

As I've mentioned earlier, my mother was a very attractive woman, and she believed her value came from her looks. So, even though I'd had a horrific experience with lap band surgery, she decided to do the same.

Based on her health history, the surgeon shouldn't have taken her on as a patient. Mom had been sick my whole life; in fact, her severe asthma was the reason we moved from Kansas City to Arizona when I was a kid.

Later, she was diagnosed with lupus, arthritis, and other ailments. In other words, she was compromised. She was also paying cash, which meant no insurance involvement and, therefore, no accountability.

All I will say is that we decided as a family not to file a lawsuit. We certainly could have. Indeed, she was very weak after the surgery, and her condition would continue to rapidly deteriorate over the next few months.

One day in October, I came home from a Target run, set down a case of bottled water on the floor, and grabbed groceries to put in the fridge, something I had done countless times before.

Only this time, I tripped on the case. The type of fracture to my foot, called a Jones fracture, is caused by twisting and happens to a lot of athletes and dancers. On the foot, it notoriously takes longer to heal because there is not a lot of blood flow there.

I was placed in a full leg cast, which was angled at the bottom so I couldn't stand properly, let alone walk. I rode a scooter around, which wasn't much use in my two-story home. It was eighteen steps up and eighteen steps down, on my arms. Oh, and this would continue for eighteen months.

If I had known anything about angel numbers back then, I would have read that eighteen signifies "the completion of a cycle and the beginning of a new one, and that one should trust in divine process and have patience."

If I knew about the bible, I would have learned that the number eighteen signifies bondage. That I would have been able to relate to, given my limited movement. But I didn't know or care about any of that. All I knew was that this SUCKED.

Shortly after I broke my foot, the doctors diagnosed Mom with "failure to thrive," which in adults includes a host of symptoms like decreased appetite, depression, and impaired immune function.

She was also unable to keep anything down, just as I'd been after my stomach surgery, but much more severe, and she needed a feeding tube. Inserting it, the doctors said, was a fairly simple procedure; they would go in through the jugular. Instead, they were unable to do that, and Mom ended up in the ICU, even worse off than before.

I will never forget the moment when my mother looked me in the eye and said, "Help me." I knew they were the last words she would ever speak to me, yet I felt powerless to do anything but place my trust in the doctors.

Mom never got strong enough to have the surgery, so they sent her home on hospice. There, she went seventeen days without food or water before she passed.

She had a really strong heart.

She was also only sixty-four.

I was devastated by my mother's decline and death. I raged at the injustice of it all, the botched surgery, the irresponsibility of the surgeon. I was also carrying the weight of the things I experienced throughout my relationship with her.

From the time I was a little girl, I was seen as a reflection of her, so if I gained weight, had no makeup on, or didn't have curly hair, I wasn't perfect, and neither was she. The damage caused by this had manifested as drug use and promiscuity when I was a teen.

Much later, as I reflected and peeled back the layers, I was able to see my mother and the circumstances of her death from a place of truth. She died *because* she didn't love herself, and she died *never* having known self-love.

Yes, the surgeon may have done the wrong thing, but the events were set in motion by her choice to have a procedure that would improve her appearance. Most importantly, I would realize that for my entire life, my mother had been teaching me what a lack of self-love looked like, so I could wake up and make a different choice.

> *When we learn to love ourselves unconditionally, we can love others in the same way. We can maintain our energy while loving them. This love is based on respect, energetically and physically, and is free of judgment and obligation.*

How do you begin to shift into this higher perspective? First, you have to want it. For me, that wanting began with the realization that I was repeating this pattern with my own kids. I did not love my sons unconditionally, and I wanted to. I also remembered longing to be free of responsibility for my mother's happiness, and I refused to place that burden on Dennis and Billy's shoulders. I wanted them to *want* to be with me, rather than feeling they *had* to.

If you are thinking of your own family and asking, "Why does it have to be me? Why is it my job to break these cycles?" you are not alone. If you often wonder, "Why does it seem everyone is losing their shit?" it's because the energy, ours and the Earth's, is shifting. Humanity is opening its heart. We are realizing that it doesn't feel good not to love somebody, to see them as "other." We are also realizing where we have not loved ourselves, and how much pain that has caused us and those around us.

This energy shift means it's time for all the outdated systems— the banks, governments, schools, and churches—to change. As we do this work, we learn to tune out the noise of these systems; we are less distracted and more present in our bodies.

Those systems are like the ego. They have served a purpose, but their time of control is ending. And, like the ego, they will protect themselves by trying to pull us out of the body and back into the confusion. Just know that we can always come back to center.

MEETING SUNNY

Before I dive into one of the most pivotal moments on my path, let me introduce you to the woman who would help me begin to truly remember who I am. Sunny Dawn Johnston is a psychic medium, spiritual teacher, and author based in Phoenix—the same desert I call home.

From the moment I met her, I knew our paths were meant to intertwine. I didn't know how or why, but I felt it in my bones. Looking back, I can say without question that Sunny has been one of the greatest catalysts for my transformation.

Her presence gave me permission to explore, unravel, and unlearn—without judgment. She never gave me answers, but always pointed me back to my own truth. Through her teachings, her example, and her unwavering love, she has offered me hope, clarity, and the space to remember who I came here to be. I will be forever grateful.

The first time I met Sunny, I showed up with a notebook, a pen, and an attitude.

"I don't believe in any of this," I told her, "but I've been guided here, so tell me what I need to learn."

Sunny didn't miss a beat. "Your guides are banging their heads against the wall right now. They're saying, 'It took you long enough to get here.' You also have a whole bunch of people here who are so glad you've come."

She then proceeded to describe a "feisty little woman"—under five feet tall and about ninety pounds—who I immediately knew to be my great-grandmother, Ruth.

I didn't know what to make of that. I still couldn't believe I was even speaking with a psychic medium and spiritual teacher. On the other hand, I could not deny the things (I would not have called them "synchronicities" back then) that had happened since my mom's passing a couple of years earlier.

I missed her, and that emotion, coupled with these "things," made me curious enough to investigate further. Later, I would recognize this as the beginning, a slight opening up to realities beyond the physical world.

It started immediately after she died, when a bird flew to the window and pressed its beak to the glass. And, in that moment, I felt the possibility that it was connected to Mom or was a message of some kind. It wasn't belief—nothing like that—but more like, *Isn't that interesting ...?*

The next thing was what I could only describe as a response to a request I sent out. I had recognized that with my broken foot and advocating for Billy, I was unable to care for my father the way I wanted to and thought he deserved.

This awareness that I could not take on one more thing was, in and of itself, a change for me; much more significant was that I *acted on it* by saying to Spirit or Mom—I didn't know who—"I need help, I cannot do this on my own."

The speed with which that help arrived shocked me as much as the form it took: Dad met someone. As he told me the news, I remember focusing, not on the woman's name (Joyce), her age (she was just ten years older than me), or even the fact that he was dating so soon, but the name of the restaurant she owned: Cici's. CiCi was the name my mom was called by her grandchildren. She had never wanted to be called Grandma; she was too young and pretty for that. There had already been a Mimi and a GiGi in the family, so Mom became CiCi. When I heard this, I had a feeling of connection, of being heard.

I reminded myself of all this when, a couple of months later, I learned that Joyce would be moving in with Dad. Having her there would be good for him and lift a responsibility from my shoulders (exactly what I had asked for).

This, coupled with the odd CiCi "coincidence," helped me accept a situation that normally would have upset me. It was as if my mother had delivered the assistance, or at least approved of it. This was the space I was in when my sister Buffy and I went to clean out Mom's closet, which had remained untouched since her passing.

It was surreal, for sure, to pull up to our parents' large, beautiful home knowing the difficult task that lay ahead, and that our family was starting a new chapter without Mom. Dad and Joyce were away on vacation, giving us space to work.

It's not unusual to see enormous walk-in closets in Arizona homes—many are like sitting rooms, part of the master bedroom suite. Mom's, however, was on a whole other level—completely color coordinated and organized into outfits. Some even had scarves and jewelry attached to them. It looked like a department store, which was why my sister had flown in to help.

So I was taken aback when we walked in and the first thing I noticed, sticking out among the color-coded shirts, was a white T-shirt. It was the kind of shirt you would see at a state fair, with what looked to be some sort of gimmicky cartoon on it. To understand how odd this was, you'd have to know a little more about my mom.

She was very proper and had a classic look—lots of Ralph Lauren shirts, all with collars (and sometimes shoulder pads), all perfectly ironed. I rarely saw her without "her face" on; she applied her makeup first thing in the morning, and her hair was always perfect. This wasn't the kind of mom to get in the pool with the kids. In other words, she was everything I'm not, and she *certainly* never wore T-shirts.

I walked over to this T-shirt—a Hanes, no less!—and picked it up to see a decal of George W. Bush looking back at me. He was in the Oval Office, and beneath the picture were the words, "Miss me yet?" This was also strange, because my family doesn't do politics, though I did know, of course, that he had been out of office for years.

And in that moment, I just knew the "Miss me yet?" was a message from Mom.

Isn't that interesting …

After three days of going through a seemingly endless supply of clothes, bags, wigs, belts, and scarves, sorting what would be donated and so on, Buffy and I pretty much had everything done.

I drove her to the airport, then returned to the house with Clorox wipes. There was another round of donations to deliver, plus I wanted to wipe down the shelves and clear out the hangers.

That's when I saw the ring, sitting on one of the shelves. I recognized it immediately.

Mom was crazy about jewelry and had quite a collection; my parents enjoyed going on cruises, and she often came back with something new from one port or another. She was very proud of the pieces Dad bought her and liked to show them off. This ring had been one of her favorites, and I remembered when she lost it. For several years before she passed, she'd started forgetting things and sometimes misplacing them as well. The ring stood out because of how devastated she was when it went missing; I'm not even certain she told my dad about it.

Now, there it was, as if waiting for me to find it. As if Mom was trying, with the T-shirt and the ring, to let me know she was around. I didn't know how she could orchestrate a bird pressing its beak against the window or my dad meeting someone who owned a place called Cici's, but those things were marinating in my mind as well.

Again, this was only a slight opening. I still wasn't sold on any of it. This isn't the point in the story where I renounced my atheistic ways, started chanting mantras, and embraced Spirit.

I did share a bit with my friend Laura, whom I had known since high school. I trusted her, but when she mentioned how a woman named Sunny Dawn Johnston had helped her process the traumatic death of her four-year-old niece, I dismissed the idea of meeting her. I wasn't interested, I said, and I meant it.

Two months later, my son and I had some time before an appointment and randomly stopped at a nearby gift shop. When I saw a book called *The Love Never Ends* by Sunny Dawn Johnston, I thought, *Well, that's interesting.* Again, no epiphany, no commitment. Then I walked around the corner and saw silver rings with a silver tray in the middle that read Sherry—my mom's name. I bought it and *The Love Never Ends*, devoured the book in one sitting, and then reached out to Laura for Sunny's information.

I didn't buy into anything at that first meeting, but I did listen to what Sunny said (none of it made much sense) and took a lot of notes. More importantly, I felt that immediate connection with Sunny, that same feeling of home I had experienced when I met Dennis. When she spoke, I heard a ring of truth.

Looking back, I can see the breadcrumbs Spirit had laid out, and how each step was gently leading me to this woman who would walk beside me for years to come. Sunny has never once told me what to believe. Instead, she has reminded me—over and over again—that everything I need is already within me. She has helped me reclaim my voice, my truth, and my light. I'll never be able to fully express the depth of my gratitude for the role she has played in my healing.

But I'm getting ahead of myself. There was still a lot I had to go through before I could fully receive what she came here to mirror. First, I had to make the decision to stay.

Because every experience—every heartbreak, every trauma, every choice—was preparing me to embody the Light. To love myself, not in spite of it all ... but because of it.

FREE FALL

T he first movie my husband and I ever saw together was *The Game*. For those of you who haven't seen it, I apologize for the spoiler alert. Michael Douglas plays an investment banker whose brother gives him a rather unusual birthday present. It is an experience, a game, an opportunity for adventure, which he turns down because he is too busy, too important … and, though he doesn't know it, too broken.

The game proceeds anyway, and he is taken on a roller coaster ride in which everything that has haunted him (including his father's suicide) is excavated and revisited for him to overcome. People he has always trusted completely abandon him, while others come into his life, seemingly for the express purpose of causing his demise. Everything he had clung to, his wealth, his sense of control, is crumbling.

At several points, he is presented with a choice: does he face his circumstances head-on, or does he check out like his father had? In the end, he realizes it has all been an illusion, a game; everything he went through was an opportunity for expansion, an invitation to awaken.

That movie is one of, if not the best, metaphors for life I have found. I also find it interesting that my husband and I saw it together. It's as if Spirit was giving us a glimpse of the future and its own sense of humor.

Let me explain.

Each incarnation on Earth, we are given opportunities—designed by Spirit, our spirit team, and our Higher Selves—for our growth and evolution. Everyone in our lives, from our dearest confidants to our worst enemies, is acting as our teachers. We are all playing roles in each other's "game." It is always our choice to take those opportunities or not, and to see others' actions from a higher perspective or at the level of the "ant farm."

In 2016, after seventeen months and my foot still unhealed, I opted to have the stem cell surgery presented to me by a hip sports medicine surgeon. There would be no more limping around in that big boot or riding a scooter. In this procedure, they take amniotic fluid from a donor and inject it into the bone to promote growth and healing. It was all the rage at the time, and, for many people, it works great. For others, it activates the inflammatory system because they are taking on someone else's DNA.

No one told me that this procedure, while simple, also carries the same risks as an organ transplant. I had no idea that what was being sold as a "solution" would turn into my biggest nightmare.

Within a week of the surgery, my health went into a free-fall. It began with a full-body rash that made me feel as though I was on fire. The crown of my head felt "concaved" inward and was so red, hot, raw, and tender I couldn't even touch it, let alone brush my hair. Not that it mattered, because the fatigue was so debilitating I couldn't lift the brush to my head. Sometimes, it felt like an effort just to breathe. It hurt to think. It was as if all the life force energy had been drained from me.

I immediately sought help from any doctors I thought might be able to help. My only frame of reference at that time was the Western medicine model I'd grown up with (i.e., Dr. Spock knew everything and antibiotics could cure almost anything).

To get to those doctors, I had to jump through several hoops. I had to find one who would see me (usually, I saw the nurse practitioner first) and give me a referral to a specialist and then another, and another, and so on.

There were also many times when I went to urgent care or the emergency room because I was so sick and not getting help. They always thought I was seeking pain medication (though I never requested it), which made me feel like a drug addict and uncomfortable seeking care.

What I got was a game of whack-a-mole. Every part of my body was affected, but none of the symptoms seemed related. Unable to figure out what was wrong, the doctors would chalk them up to something else.

When I lost my hearing in one ear, they said, "Oh, it must have been an upper respiratory infection." I knew this was wrong—I'd had countless upper respiratory infections in my life and never lost my hearing. Yet, there I was, wearing a hearing aid. What choice did I have? I also received a dozen other diagnoses and recommendations for painful surgical procedures. I was looked down upon when I said no. Yet, I remained determined to find the root cause.

By far, the most unbearable thing was my eyes. I had been through so many awful, even life-threatening, health crises, and nothing compared to this. The burning was so bad it felt like acid was being thrown on me, and I lived in fear that I would lose my vision at any minute. Even the smallest bit of light caused excruciating pain, so much so that for months I stayed in the house with the shades drawn and wore big black glasses and a hat.

I underwent every test possible, all of them ruling things out but not telling me anything. At first, the best explanation the eye specialists could come up with was "dry eye." Then, because there was quite a bit of discharge, they decided it might help to plug my tear ducts, which only locked in the toxicity that my body was trying to purge.

My ultimate goal was to get in with an infectious disease specialist. I just knew there were toxins in my system, something foreign that was causing an infection. Piece by piece, my body was shutting down.

And, like most people with chronic illness, when I wasn't going from doctor to doctor or searching for a new one, I was spending every last ounce of my limited energy on researching my symptoms and the possible connections between them. I left no stone unturned, yet at the same time, I was still relying on allopathic doctors for answers and healing.

If my eye symptoms were the most painful, the most terrifying were cognitive. I would go to say something and find myself searching for the right words; I had always been a great writer, but now I couldn't even compose an email. It's as if the thoughts were right there, floating above my head, and I couldn't "pull them down."

A part of me felt untethered as well. I struggled to stay present even for the briefest conversation; focusing on anything longer, like a TV show or a movie, was out of the question.

At my son's weekly indoor soccer games, I would sit on a bench, eyes closed behind my shades to minimize light exposure, and hear my family cheering him on as if through a long tunnel. It was as if I were locked within myself, unable to get to them.

After eleven months of medical tests, red tape, and internet searches, I finally got an appointment with an infectious disease doctor. In the meantime, my condition had continued to rapidly deteriorate, and so had my hope.

The moment she walked into the room, along with some colleagues, I felt a spark of that hope return. She was dressed in a tie-dye shirt and Birkenstocks, and her demeanor as she greeted me was laid back yet engaged. If I could have conjured a doctor who most resonated with me at that time, it would have been someone who looked like her.

Finally, I thought, *Finally, I am going to get answers. Finally, I am going to be heard.*

You know what they say about looks, folks. Once I started discussing my symptoms, her attitude completely shifted. She dismissed everything I said and, after just a few minutes, told her colleagues they could leave, as if what I was saying wasn't worthy of their time.

Not knowing where else to turn, I continued to see her for several months. She ran test after test, including one for drugs, and found the presence of Epstein-Barr and cytomegalovirus.

After telling me they "weren't a big deal," she promptly ordered a full psychological evaluation. This wasn't like, "Go talk to a counselor," but a grueling, eight-hour day during which I was completely at their mercy, meaning they could have decided to commit me, and there wouldn't have been a fucking thing I could do about it.

They determined that I was perfectly sane, though they did diagnose me with situational high anxiety over the medical issue, as well as severe ADHD. It was the only useful piece of information to come out of that day.

The results of the psych eval had no effect on "Dr. Birkenstocks," who then decided that I was a bored housewife seeking attention from my husband. She literally said those words, not only to her colleagues but to Dennis, all of whom accepted her assumptions without question.

I recall that last meeting with her, when she laid it all on me. I felt ridiculed, powerless, and so sick I couldn't even summon the strength to defend myself. Why, after everything I had already been through, was I led to this woman who had shown up exactly like "my girl," only to rip my soul right out of my chest?

Sometimes we feel like we have hit rock bottom, only to realize we have further to fall.

That happened in the car ride home, when my husband turned to me and said, "Are you going to let this go now?"

What I took this to mean was, "Are we going to stop talking about this now? Are we going to focus on more important things?"

This was the man I had known I was going to marry the night we met, because he felt like "home." And, for the last twenty years, he had been. He was my partner, my backbone, my support. Now that same man was saying he agreed with the doctor, that this was all in my head, that the "jig was up."

That was rock bottom. That was the moment I knew I was truly on my own.

And on my own is where I would find my own power. It was where I needed to be.

WE ALL PLAY EVERY ROLE

Recently, someone asked my husband when I began to heal. His response: "When she lost faith in me."

Taken at face value, these words can be seen as self-blame and regret, and surely he has felt that. But on a deeper level, and with the greater awareness he now has, he was describing his role in a divinely orchestrated plan—his part in "my game," and my part in his.

He is also referring to a very dark time in our marriage. When, after that last doctor's appointment, I didn't "let it go" as he'd suggested, he began what felt like a very cruel campaign against me. He would insinuate that I was crazy. He completely dismissed my worsening symptoms and reminded me that the doctors knew best.

I would say to him, "Come here, feel this," gesturing to the hot spot at the crown of my head.

"No," he would say, as if not seeing that angry, hot, red area. "It's always been there."

He also let me know, in subtle and passive-aggressive ways, that he was watching me and might be forced to take action if I did anything that appeared outside the norm. I never knew what that action was, but I was always afraid of losing my sons. I was even very careful about what I searched online; I was doing a lot of research on my symptoms and anything that could possibly help me, and I didn't want him to see that.

During this time, it was as if I were being tortured on all fronts. Everyone knows how uncomfortable it is to have something in their eye—be it an eyelash, a pet hair, or sleep when they get up in the morning. Everyone knows how frustrating it is to try to get it out, with their eye getting redder and more irritated.

Now imagine that something feels like pieces of glass, and it continues for months. All the while, you feel like you're under surveillance in your own home, and you're being told that it's all in your mind. In addition to the pain, you feel shame, you want to hide, and you think you may be going crazy after all.

I remember saying, "If you knew how much pain I'm in right now, you wouldn't be treating me like this. You would be helping me. I can't explain it either. I don't know what the fuck is wrong!"

The gaslighting continued. There were even times when he took his phone out and recorded how "ridiculous" I was acting.

Did he reconsider when my hair began noticeably thinning, then fell out altogether? I had no idea, but if he did, he said nothing.

Worse yet, he told our sons, who were in elementary and middle school at the time, that I wasn't sick, that I didn't need to go to the doctors. This was very difficult for them to reconcile, considering they often saw me unable to get out of bed. I was terrified that he would take them away from me or that they would grow to resent me. I didn't feel emotionally safe in our home.

My entire life, I had been looking outside of me—to the education system, the medical system, the news media, and to my husband—for answers and support. And when that doctor showed up as my savior and then wasn't, and when my husband, who had always been my rock, was no longer so, I was completely crushed. Everything was stripped away, everything but me and my choice. I could lie down and die, or I could get up and fight.

I freely admit that at first, I tried to lie down and die. For so long, I had been alone and in pain and so very, very exhausted, and there was no end in sight.

This was not depression—I had been depressed before and knew what that felt like. This was complete despair—physically, mentally, emotionally, and spiritually. It was thinking my family would be better off without me.

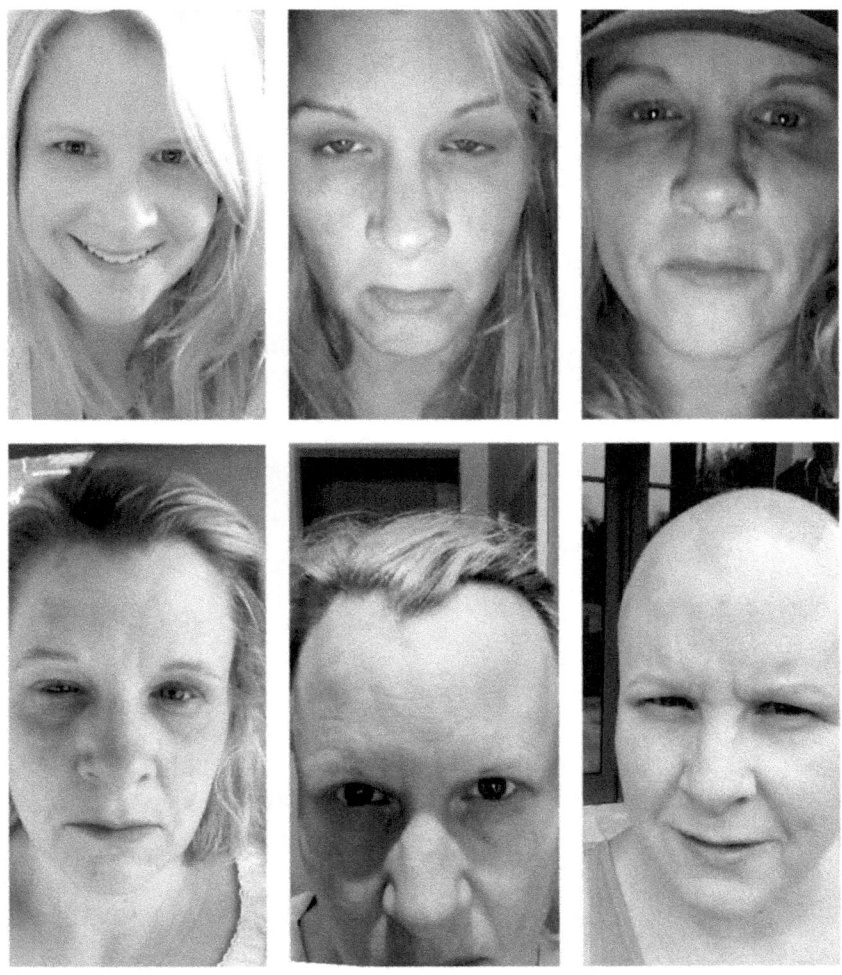

Yes, part of me was still waiting for a cure, but that part was getting smaller and smaller, while the larger part, the part that was preparing to leave, was growing. If this was the way life was going to be, I was going to find a way out, even if that meant doing it on my own.

It was in this space that I sat down and wrote letters to my sons. I wrote about how much I loved them and the other usual things one writes under these circumstances. But, in part, I wrote them to defend myself. I was going to die—I felt I had no choice about that—but I could let them know that I really had been sick, that I had fought so hard to stay with them, even though it didn't look like it on the outside. I wanted them to know I hadn't just given up. With every fucking breath, I had fought to stay with them.

With that, I completely surrendered and waited to die.

Only … I didn't.

> *I didn't understand that this was just a transition period. While in this solitary confinement, dissociated and in pain, I was also preparing to meet my higher self. I had to get the energetic debris, accumulated over my life, out of the way so I could begin to integrate. In surrendering and in writing those letters, I moved the energy of fear and guilt about leaving my boys out of my body. I went inside and opened my heart, really felt my feelings. And, in doing so, I was beginning that very, very introductory relationship with Spirit. I was opening myself up to healing on all levels.*

It was around this time that I also began to feel anger toward my husband. I started telling myself, "I deserve better than this. This is not what love looks like."

People, especially those in the spiritual community, see anger as an indicator of emotional unhealthiness. We are raised to think it's impolite; it offends or hurts others; it doesn't solve anything. This is not entirely accurate.

*Like all emotions, anger is neither good nor bad. It is sim-
ply energy that needs to move. It can also be motivating and
empowering. It is all about what we choose to do with it.*

Anger was definitely an improvement over the powerlessness I
had felt, in some form or another, my whole life—as a child, forced
to sleep in curlers and perform for the catwalk and cameras; during
the sexual assaults in college and my addictions to substances and
unhealthy people.

Later, I felt powerless through infertility and the ectopic pregnancy that nearly killed me. I felt it when I gave up my career in
law enforcement, and when I was unable to take Billy's struggles
from him. I felt it when the bottom dropped out of my health, and
I had to beg "experts," who didn't even believe me, for answers. And
those were just some of the most prominent examples of an energetic thread running through my experience.

Like all emotions, anger is neither positive nor negative. If we hold
onto it, it becomes toxic; when we understand energy, we can use it
as a catalyst. Within the context of my marriage, anger fueled me. It
led me to *want* to feel worthy. And, though I was not in a space of
wanting to leave my marriage, just *imagining* myself as healthy enough
to do so was a form of hope. It was about reaching a point where I
would be willing to walk myself out of any situation where I was being
wronged. That's when Spirit showed me another way.

*Everything that had happened—all the crises leading up to
my illness, the illness itself, and the reactions of those around
me were meant to happen for my growth and transformation.
Part of this transformation was understanding and taking
accountability for the way I had shown up in my relationships.*

When I connected with Spirit, I began to see all of this from a
higher, very different perspective. I remembered the resentment I

had felt about my mother being sick my whole life. Everything I did when I was growing up revolved around my mom, what she was able to do, and how she was going to feel.

So when she started getting sick, I didn't understand how someone could be sick all the time. There is now more recognition of "invisible" diseases, but that wasn't the case then. I have vivid memories of being in the hospital with her, especially the last couple years of her life. And my words were, "Well, Mom, if something were wrong, the tests would show it."

When she said things like, "Something's wrong. My brain's not working right," I thought—though I didn't say this to her—that maybe she had the beginnings of dementia. I also remember rolling my eyes and placating her like a child when, several months before her death, she told me that her father in spirit had visited her.

This was no easy pill to swallow, especially since I now knew how it felt to be dismissed and diminished by those we're looking to for love and support. I had been the doubter, the one who, because I couldn't control the situation and make it better, said things that had the effect of gaslighting her.

I had played the same role with her as my husband had played with me.

Part of my work then was finding compassion and empathy for myself and for the way I had shown up with my mother. This was deeper than forgiving myself and trying to push down my guilt by listing all the ways I had been a *good* daughter. It was understanding that when I had dismissed her, I was operating from my level of awareness at the time. So, wasn't the same true for my husband? Didn't he deserve the same grace I was giving myself?

I began to see him as a human.

Sunny was instrumental in this. Through our mentorship, she helped me understand that our partner isn't supposed to be our end-all, be-all. We are trained to think this way and believe that having a partner means we will always be safe and supported.

This is why many people who don't have a partner feel less-than or incomplete. Those who do have a partner and still feel so isolated and alone experience a loss of expectations. I had an expectation that my husband would be able to support me financially, emotionally, spiritually, and mentally. When those expectations are not met, where do we go to feel safe? We go within. We go to Spirit.

Each of us has gifts and things we are strong in, and each of us has things we need help with. My husband didn't do well at not being able to fix things. He also didn't have a lot of empathy or compassion for himself, and as a result, he didn't have a lot to give others. He saw me and our sons as a kind of projection of himself, and so unknowingly was holding us to the same standard he held himself to. That standard was to be strong, don't feel, don't show weakness.

I had been fixated on the one thing he didn't do—not because he didn't want to, but because he wasn't able to at that time. As I shifted my perspective, I was able to find gratitude for everything he *had* been doing: working full-time to support us, and taking care of the kids, the house, and the dogs when I was unable to do any of it. He had been Superman, not just during the illness, but for the year and a half my foot was broken.

I also reflected on my behavior, including my deep dive into Dr. Google, with whom I spent much of my time while obsessively searching for a cure, and I saw how concerning that must have been for him.

His actions were not coming from malice, but rather a fear of losing me and the shame and powerlessness he felt over not being able to help.

This is not about excusing or accepting hurtful behavior. It's about understanding that we can maintain our own energy in the face of it and show up differently in response to it. This invites the other person to evolve as well.

My husband wasn't aware of any of this—not my inner work or that I was mentally preparing to have a conversation with him about the future of our relationship. In the meantime, I was completely focused on my physical healing and rebuilding my energy so I could rejoin the living.

Then, once I was connected to Spirit, I often felt like I was walking in a dream. I certainly didn't have the words or understanding of what was happening to explain it to another. Learning was my first priority.

For two years, I felt like I was living two lives; I was playing two parts. As I started working with Sunny, I slowly became stronger, more empowered, and confident. I learned how to express myself and speak my truth. Yet, I hadn't shared it with Dennis because I didn't want to hurt him. He really had tried his hardest; also, I could see how easy it was to believe the doctors as they ran test after test. I had also rediscovered my gratitude for all the years he *had* been my backbone.

It was 2019 when I decided the time was right to speak with him. It was the only way for us to move forward, and for me to release the significant trauma I was still carrying about the experience. Sharing this was the next step of my growth, and given the state of our relationship, I believed I would feel more heard if I wrote it out.

It was a tool we had learned in counseling twenty years earlier. "Written communication is better than no communication," our counselor had said. "If letters are what you guys are more comfortable with for hard conversations, that's okay."

This gave me permission to express myself in ways I had been unable to when I felt intimidated, dismissed, or gaslit.

My letter to him was all "I statements." I shared how hurt I was feeling, but rather than talking about anything he had done, I wrote only about what I'd come to recognize about myself. The illness wasn't anybody's fault; it was something that happened to us. However, I also made it clear that we'd gone through a transition and had both changed because of it. I was a very different person than I once was, and I took complete responsibility for that change.

The difference was that, at this time, *I was choosing me more.* No longer was I doing everything for everybody. I also shared that I'd finally found what I was looking for in the spiritual teachings and community, that I felt seen and heard.

Most importantly, I now understood what I was meant to do: share my story of healing with others, so they could expand, grow, and heal themselves. My purpose and passion were to continue speaking my truth. I could do that on my own, or I could do that with him; the choice was his.

He chose to grow and expand. Dennis understood and celebrated the fact that I had stepped into my purpose. Many people, he noted, spend their whole lives searching for that and never find it.

I'm deeply grateful to him for playing his part in my awakening so perfectly—for holding space, giving me room to evolve, and encouraging me as I stepped into my healing. His willingness to grow alongside me opened the door to a more intimate partnership, a stronger marriage, and a united family rooted in truth and love. He chose to expand, and that marked the rebirth of our relationship.

That doesn't mean it was all sunshine and rainbows. Like the rest of this journey, there was beauty and joy, but it was also really hard and sometimes it just plain sucked. He felt awful about the way he showed up, and he has had to do the same forgiveness work that I had done when I realized the role I had played with my mother.

Could this have gone down a different way? Absolutely. As you grow and you shed your skin, you may also find yourself shedding people. Sometimes that is necessary, and sometimes that is taking the easy way out. It takes practice to discern the difference. It means pulling back and looking at the totality of a relationship. It means looking in the mirror and being honest with yourself, no holds barred, while also having radical acceptance, love, and compassion for what you see.

It takes work every day to show up and have self-awareness and presence and self-reflection, to ask, "Okay, what is my part in this?

How did I contribute to this situation?" Because I now know, without a doubt, that I manifested that illness—yes, for my own expansion, but also to get attention and for a variety of other reasons.

I never would have imagined during that awful period how people could come back together and in a stronger way than ever before. BUT/AND, it took my willingness to get *really* real, and my husband's willingness, as the person who was not in touch with their emotions and was "in the wrong," to open his heart and listen.

People can change and grow, just as my family did. But it was never me telling them what they should do or what they should listen to. It doesn't work like that. We can't control it like that. He and my children had to see and feel the shift in me.

They witnessed what it was like to own our power. To embody our Light and our truth. To feel strong in our body and make choices that are new, uncomfortable, and facilitate growth.

Most importantly, they witnessed how we can change patterns, including those that were passed down to us. I had to do all of that so that they could see that's how it worked.

I've often thought that what happened between us is what's happening now in the collective: women are walking the men to higher awareness, to different states of being. By doing the work and showing up for ourselves, we are giving permission to the men to start to feel.

As humans, we are moving away from the patriarchal system, with its intimidating energy, and moving toward softer, gentler energy. We are returning to harmony. This is not about bashing men or saying that women are better. It is about balancing those energies so there is more collaboration, unity, and compassion.

None of us is "better" or "chosen"; however, some do have a plan, orchestrated by Spirit and our Higher Self, to go first.

We are in the trenches. We're doing the heavy lifting. And we're anchoring in the light for others to join us.

SPENDING MY HUSBAND'S MONEY

As mentioned earlier, sometime between my mother's passing in 2014 and my own downward spiral, I had begun having experiences that defied all logic and challenged my notion of reality.

The bird at the window and the T-shirt and ring in her closet turned out to be precursors to a visit from Mom herself. Of course, I had heard of mediums before, but like everything spiritual, I had dismissed them as BS. But I could not so easily dismiss my awareness of her energy around me, or the message she communicated that I had Lyme disease.

What made this even harder to ignore was the timing. The message came late one night while I was sitting outside in the backyard with my dogs, something I did often during that season of my life.

Those quiet, desperate nights under the stars were when I would plead for answers, for relief, for something—anything—that would help me understand what was happening to my body and mind. That night, I felt her presence so clearly, and the words came not as a voice but as a knowing—Lyme disease.

It resonated immediately, especially given my family's history with autoimmune issues. I even brought it up a few weeks later at an infectious disease appointment. They ran a standard antibody test, which came back negative.

At the time, I didn't know that antibody tests can give false negatives if you haven't yet received treatment—your immune system doesn't produce enough antibodies early on to register as "positive." So I dismissed it, chalked it up to wishful thinking or maybe misinterpreting signs I was too emotionally invested in.

It would take years, and many more whispers from Spirit, before I fully understood what my body had been trying to say all along. But that moment in the backyard? That was one of the very first times I received clear guidance from my mom in Spirit. Even though I didn't fully trust what I was receiving at the time, it was the beginning of a new relationship with her—one that continued to unfold long after she left her physical body.

While Western medicine focuses on Lyme as a tick-borne illness and gives little acknowledgment to its coinfections, it is, in fact, under the autoimmune, inflammatory umbrella, along with lupus, fibromyalgia, MS, rheumatoid arthritis, and several other illnesses. The name is not as important as that they all start from the same root. *It is all the same energy, manifesting differently in different people, based on their genetics, life experience, emotions, and so on.*

A determination of Lyme would mean that was how that energy finally spoke up in my body. It had been fibromyalgia ten years earlier, but I did nothing about it; if I had continued to do nothing, it could have moved toward MS. So you see, these things all kind of feed and morph into one another.

A good comparison is mental health challenges like depression, anxiety, and bipolar disorder. They all have the same start, but then they can go off in different ways. And just like those things, inflammatory illnesses are passed down from generation to generation; for example, Lyme has been scientifically proven to pass from mother to child through the placenta.[2]

---

[2] "Congenital Lyme," Project Lyme, August 7, 2024, https://projectlyme.org/resource/congenitallyme/#:~:text=Most%20of%20us%20have%20learned,Category.

Illnesses are frequencies. We manifest them when our bodies are vibrating at the same frequency. They can also be opportunities, with our Higher Selves guiding us, to clean house, to transmute that energy. A lot of us are learning to release energy that no longer serves us; as we do so, we expand and bring in more Light. Even Covid, which is different because it was meant to lower the frequency of many beings, is being used by those who have already activated their Light as a transmutation tool.

Another message from Mom—"I did it for you"—was harder to wrap my mind around. What was she talking about? What had she done for me? Was this even real?

It *felt* real, just like the massive angelic presence I saw—Statue of Liberty ginormous—who appeared before me and then disappeared in a blink. That's how this energy works: it moves in and out of form. You *see* something, *feel* something, but then doubt rushes in.

Did that really happen? Did I imagine it? Am I losing it?

It is easy to question everything, especially when your body is sick, your mind is foggy, and you're not thinking clearly. That was exactly where I was—struggling, searching, trying to hold on to whatever threads of clarity I could find.

But over time, I came to understand what she meant by "I did it for you." She was talking about her death.

At first, that idea felt cold … even cruel. Why would she say something like that?

Eventually, I realized it wasn't said with any malice or regret—it was truth. Her soul had played a role, one I wouldn't begin to grasp until I'd gone through the fire myself. Her passing cracked me open. It forced me to question everything I thought I knew, everything I believed. It triggered the unraveling of a version of myself that had to be dismantled in order to uncover the truth of who I really am.

She played her part perfectly—not as punishment, not to hurt me, but to help wake me up. Only she hadn't fully understood it at the time either.

> *That's the paradox of this human journey. Sometimes, we agree to play roles in each other's lives that only make sense later, from a higher perspective. Her leaving was the beginning of my remembering. Her departure allowed me to finally arrive—in my own life, my healing, my path. While it would still take time, pain, and many more messages to fully land, "I did it for you" became one of the most sacred truths I've ever received.*

In those early days, I spent most of my waking moments as I always had, going through the motions without being intentional or present. We often refer to this as "being on autopilot." Then, every once in a while, something would cross my path that made me perk up and notice. It was enough to make me a little curious and perhaps say, "What if …?"

Although I didn't understand it at the time, I now know I was energetically searching for more signs from my mom, which made me more present and aware. When we are in this energy, even for brief moments, it is easier to tap into higher vibrations and receive, be it something material or information. This is the essence of the law of attraction, in which we feel a desire for something, then release resistance to it (this is the openness piece), which allows it to flow in.

Of course, I wasn't sharing any of this with anyone, and I wouldn't for a very long time. Even when I eventually started seeing Sunny, I told my husband it was so she could help me deal with the loss of my mom. In fact, I was telling myself the same thing because I didn't understand why I was going down this path. Grieving for my mother was "acceptable."

I knew I wasn't going crazy, and yet I also knew my brain wasn't working properly due to whatever systemic illness was in my body. Again, I knew that toxins and a host of bacteria, fungi, parasites, and heavy metals were present, making it difficult to focus on the simplest of tasks.

Also, I could only imagine the reaction of friends and family if I, a card-carrying atheist with a health crisis, told them I was having visions and hearing the voice of my late mother. Like, "Oh, I think I saw a guardian angel. I think my mom, who's no longer here, shared some interesting information with me the other day. I think my dog's talking to me. Isn't that cool?"

Even those things would have been more believable than at the very beginning of this journey, when much of the time Spirit communicated to me with blinking lights, streetlights, and my neighbor's lights. Yes, like Morse code, except somebody had forgotten to include the training manual.

Clean psych eval or not, they would surely think I was nuts.

Hell, *I* thought I was nuts, or at least I hoped I was. There were times I prayed that I was wrong about everything, that I was having a psychotic break, and some doctor could give me a pill. I would have happily taken it.

So, if you're thinking that all of a sudden I was like "Laaaa, I'm connected to Spirit," think again. I was not confident at all in the information that I was receiving. It felt like a toss-up. Some days, it still does. The difference is that I no longer have an attachment to it. But, for sure, back then, I would have thought I was crazy too.

So, all these things were converging on me at once. In the physical, I was going through a horrific illness and being dismissed by doctors and feeling gaslit by my husband. I was preparing for my exit from this Earth.

In an energetic sense, though I had no awareness of this, I was going through an ego death and just beginning to open to Spirit and the possibility of something beyond "the ant farm."

This is the very definition of a spiritual awakening. Whether gentle or extreme, there will be some situation or event that invites us to increase our awareness and show up differently based on that awareness. By "death of the ego," we do not mean the ego's end, but rather the end of viewing ourselves through an egoic lens. When this happens, we are able to step into more self-love and accountability for the role we have played in our own story—and the stories of others—to this point. As we learn how to do this, we are taking the first steps on the journey of ascension.

It bears repeating that when I wrote those letters to my sons, I wasn't *pretending* to surrender, nor did I even understand what surrender meant in an energetic sense. I *truly* was giving up. I *really* believed I was going to die.

Even if I had the desire to stick around feeling as awful as I did, I knew whatever was inside my body would soon completely consume it; BUT/AND, because I had been stripped of all hope and expectations of support from people around me, and had purged a lot of heavier energies through the letter writing, there was just the tiniest opening for me to become aware of a new path.

Almost immediately after I wrote those letters—maybe a week or so—Spirit placed the first breadcrumb on that path. My friend Laura, the same one who would later lead me to Sunny, told me about a naturopathic practitioner. This was a completely foreign concept to me; I mean, was this person even a "real" doctor? But when Laura mentioned that this practitioner, Dr. Yosef in Scottsdale, had helped a woman with breast implant illness, something inside me sat up and took notice.

Breast implant illness (BII), which is an immune response to the foreign objects being placed in the body, shows up much the same way my illness had, with a wide range of seemingly unrelated, vague symptoms: hair loss, brain fog, joint and muscle aches, fatigue, and so on.

More importantly, the medical community had refused to acknowledge BII as a real illness and dismissed women with these symptoms as having psychological issues. Like me, they had been gaslit and called crazy, but Dr. Yosef had looked past the usual test results and delved deeper into what was going on. It was a huge plus that he was well-versed in Western medicine and could serve as my bridge between that and naturopathy.

Just a note here, friends: breadcrumbs do not necessarily appear the way we would expect them to. They may even seem so small or inconsequential that it's easy to step over them. We have *all* stepped over them, many, many times over many lifetimes. It is when we have awareness of where we have been investing our energy and pull it back that we can center, ground, and notice these breadcrumbs.

Though I was a long way from having that level of awareness, I did make an appointment to see Dr. Yosef. In doing so, I changed the trajectory of my life.

From my very first appointment, I noticed and felt a completely different attitude and approach. Instead of having to beg to be believed, I heard from Dr. Yosef only a calm determination to get to the bottom of this.

He gave me an antibody test for Lyme disease and immediately started me on IV therapy (alternating between hydrogen peroxide and vitamin C), three times a week, for the Epstein-Barr and cytomegalovirus. Hydrogen peroxide has antiviral, antibacterial, and anti-inflammatory properties; it also increases white blood cell production, which stimulates the immune system. When the results of the antibody test came back a month later, they confirmed my mother's message, given to me a year earlier, that I had Lyme disease, and completely validated my experience and my sanity. The test results also revealed that, in addition to the Epstein-Barr and cytomegalovirus, I had seven other Lyme co-infections.

As if this wasn't enough, my bloodwork indicated the presence of heavy metals, parasites, and six different kinds of mold at "warning" levels in my body. All of these things have a host of seemingly unrelated symptoms that overlap with those of Lyme, including gastrointestinal issues, headaches, and neurological and cognitive impairment, such as joint pain, brain fog, and memory loss. These symptoms are always accompanied by extreme fatigue.

Cytomegalovirus is specifically known to cause eye issues. Those symptoms were caused by a fungal overgrowth, which explained the brief periods of relief, followed by a resurgence. Think about the fungal blooms on lakes, when the spores burst out all over the place. This also tracked when it came to the light sensitivity, as some fungi grow in darkness. When the eye doctors plugged my tear ducts, my eyes had no way of detoxing. It was like pressure building behind a dam.

When the diagnosis finally came, I didn't ask my husband how he felt—I couldn't put words in his mouth. But I imagine he was relieved. He had watched me devote years of my life, my energy, and our resources to a healing journey that made no sense to most people, including him.

I'm sure he was still skeptical, especially since the traditional medical system had failed us time and time again, and we were both just beginning to explore the world of holistic and integrative care.

For me, the diagnosis wasn't about him finally "believing" me; it was about the deep, undeniable validation that came with it. That knowing I had carried inside me for so long, that intuitive truth I couldn't shake, was now being confirmed. The overwhelm I felt (and make no mistake, it was significant) over the level of toxicity in my body was nothing compared to the sheer *relief* of finally being heard.

After years of being dismissed, misunderstood, and treated as if I were imagining it all, this was a turning point. As I began those first real steps toward wellness, the physical and spiritual pieces began to click into place in a way that was both palpable and sacred. I could feel it in my bones: this was the beginning of coming home to myself.

For the next year, three days a week, I was in Dr. Yosef's office, hooked up to IV infusions. He also put me on a strict Lyme detox protocol, including naturopathic tinctures.

The time spent in treatment didn't just detox my body. It taught me a valuable lesson about self-love, and a story I had been telling myself about my value, specifically, as a partner to Dennis.

I call this story "Spending My Husband's Money."

Throughout my illness, financial resources were never an issue; Dennis made enough money to support us, so I didn't have to work; I also had insurance that covered the tests and treatments with allopathic doctors. What wasn't covered, we could make up ourselves. This, in and of itself, was an eye-opening experience. I had all the money to see the best doctors—plus, I live in the U.S., for crying out loud!—and none of it mattered. I was still dismissed, and I was still dying.

Holistic and naturopathic healing modalities weren't covered by insurance, and making that pivot was not easy. The treatments were costly, around twenty-five thousand dollars that first year, all out of pocket. That cost included various natural healing modalities, including the care I received from Dr. Yosef. At the time, I was also becoming aware of how difficult it can be for many people to access this kind of care without insurance support, which made my own decision to invest in myself feel even more significant.

I never felt practitioners shouldn't be compensated for their supplements and treatments. *They saved my life.* I also came to understand the complexities around accepting insurance. Many holistic providers fear being shut down and losing their ability to serve because of politics, government regulations, and bureaucracy.

Bottom line: Healing is not profitable for the Western medicine system. I know this, and yet I remember the conflicted emotions, feeling incredibly blessed to be there even as I noticed how wrong this was. I also began to realize how incredibly uncomfortable I was with spending this money on myself. Without a doubt, I never would have done it if I weren't dying.

"Spending My Husband's Money" went something like this. When we got married, Dennis and I were equal partners in every way. I was the breadwinner, with a government job in law enforcement, insurance, and the promise of a pension when I retired. Dennis was always an incredibly hard worker, but at that time, he was growing his first business. I provided our stability.

That all changed when I left my job after the shooting and became a stay-at-home mom. Dennis didn't act or treat me differently in any way. Having been raised by a single mother, he knew the value and importance of that role, and he had always respected me as a mom and a homemaker, whether I was bringing home a salary or not.

However, something shifted within me. Suddenly, I was less valuable because I wasn't bringing money in. When I first got sick and for a long time after that, I didn't think about it; for one, I was desperate; for another, insurance was paying for it.

Now, I suddenly had to be okay with enormous expenditures, just for me. This brought up many uncomfortable feelings, most prominently guilt. Dennis had earned this money for the family, and now I was taking it away. I realized that while I had always been willing to spend any amount on my kids, I struggled with feeling worthy to spend on myself. As I would later come to realize, this struggle was rooted in the same lack of self-love that had led to my illness in the first place.

To truly heal from anything, we need to cultivate worth and deservingness, but how? How do you feel self-love if you have never felt it before? Again, you start by surrendering these feelings and asking for help. You learn to allow in support, to find the courage to reach for the light.

It is enough in the beginning to want it. It is saying, "I don't feel that way yet, but I will allow myself to take the steps I am guided to take, even if they are uncomfortable."

Money is a sticking point for many, if not most, people. They may have "too much" and feel shame around it, they may not have enough and feel a lack of abundance, or they may look at other people's money and judge them for it.

The issue is *never* the money; it is our energy around it that is significant. Not spending money on myself was an indication that I was not open to receive. It was another way of dimming my light. It was the same thing as not asking for help and staying in isolation. I am *not in any way* diminishing financial challenges. What I am saying is that, whether you have money or not, you will receive the breadcrumbs that will lead you to healing.

Everyone deserves healing, but not everyone will choose it.

If you are still doubting what I am saying, consider this: money did not save me when I was searching for answers or when I went to the doctors who gaslighted me. I had to take the next step to see the naturopath and be willing to love myself enough to pay for it. That willingness opened me up to receive the next breadcrumb, the man who would ultimately help me regain my health.

And he was absolutely free.

PART III

Awakening

There comes a time, often after the breaking, when something begins to stir. A quiet knowing that there is more to life than the routine you've been surviving. Not a grand revelation, but a soft curiosity: Why am I here? What else is possible?

You begin to see how you've been moving through the world, from ego, protection, or autopilot, and sense that you're more than the roles you've been playing.

Sensitivity heightens. The veil thins.

One day in the desert, everything felt alive—colors brighter, sounds louder, even the plants seemed to speak. It was as if Spirit cracked open the ordinary and let me glimpse the truth underneath.

But it wasn't all magic. My body couldn't yet move the energy, so even daily life felt overwhelming. I didn't have words for it, but I knew something was changing. I was still in the unknown.

You may find yourself reaching for answers from books, intuitive readings, or classes. They can be helpful. But eventually, the real invitation is to turn inward. To stop outsourcing your truth and start trusting your own knowing.

And when the messy stuff rises—shame, fear, regret—it's compassion that opens the door.

You're not here to do it perfectly.

You're here to remember.

To love yourself through the return.

THE BATH

If you have been on the journey for a while (and even if you haven't), you've probably heard that Spirit and Higher Self are guiding us every minute of every day that we're on this plane.

Sounds great, right? *Only if you are ready to hear and feel it.* Otherwise, it sounds like all the other empty rhetoric coming at you, every day, all the time. It becomes another "system," and like all systems, it comes with a lot of *shoulds* and *woulds.* A "spiritual" person would do this, an "enlightened" person would find the joy and see the lesson in everything from a stubbed toe to a divorce, then act on it with a smile and light shooting out of their crown chakra. There are kernels of truth in all of it, but again, just hearing those words without taking the steps will not only be unhelpful; it will likely make you incredibly angry and feel more hopeless.

That's certainly how it would have sounded to me when I was deathly ill and being written off as an attention-seeking nut. I am not discounting any knowledge you might have acquired about spiritual topics, especially if you felt called to explore them. What I am saying is that you don't need it to connect.

In my case, the less information I had from others, the better. I needed an experience that unfolded organically, with the least resistance possible coming from my ego self.

All you have to focus on is the breadcrumb in front of you ...
then the next one ... and the next. The challenge lies in doing so

without knowing where they are leading and learning to trust that it is for your evolution.

Now, imagine attending a class with Spirit. No pre-enrollment or prerequisite classes needed; the teachers are there, waiting, when you feel called to show up. There is no pressure to be anything other than who you are in that moment—flaws, fears, illnesses, whatever.

Spirit is not interested in pedigrees or certifications; it doesn't care if you've spent time at an ashram, can recite the bible by heart, or know what a Merkabah is. In fact, having less "book knowledge" actually makes it easier for your entire support team—Spirit, your Higher Self, angels, and guides—to work with you. They don't have to "undo" any faulty assumptions your human mind has made. All you need is a willingness to surrender resistance as much as you are able at that time to allow the smallest opening for the Light to come in.

That is very much what those early years were like for me. My "classroom" happened to be my bathtub. Your classroom might be the woods, the beach, or wherever you have been guided.

This "guidance" can show up in a number of ways. For example, you get the thought, *Today's a great day for a walk.* Maybe the first time you talk yourself out of going because you have too many things to do, or whatever the case may be. Maybe you're still saying that the hundredth time you get the nudge. It does not matter. The seed has been planted; you will go when you are ready, or another opportunity will be presented.

I was guided to the bath because of the hydrogen peroxide IVs I was getting at Dr. Yosef's office. They provided me with the first real hope I'd had in nearly two years; they also caused me to give off a really bad odor similar to that of rotten eggs. The hydrogen peroxide (H_2O_2) breaks down in the body into water (H_2O) and oxygen (O_2), but during this oxidative process, free radicals and reactive oxygen species are also generated. This can create byproducts that affect the body's natural detox pathways, especially the liver and lungs. The smell was so bad that my family had to open the windows.

To say this highly unpleasant side effect was a blessing in disguise doesn't even begin to cover it. A more accurate description would be a profound example of the myriad ways Spirit works to position us where we need to be, if we will allow ourselves to be guided, even if it (literally or figuratively) stinks.

That smell was what prompted me to start taking nightly baths. Like many daily activities, bathing can be seen as something that has to be done (and rushed through on autopilot), or it can be a deeply spiritual ritual.

The latter is what it would become for me; in fact, the bath was the gateway to a host of spiritual experiences and ultimately expedited my development. At this very early stage, however, when I was feeling the small spark of hope that I might actually survive, the baths were an act of self-care, perhaps the first I had ever allowed myself.

As a mother of two young children, I had placed expectations on myself to show up in a certain way, to have family dinner, help them with homework, and watch TV with them. I remember thinking that if I still had energy at the end of the day, I would do this or that, just for me.

But I never did have the energy; I never found the time. I was always last on the list. This was a story I told myself, about what having a family was supposed to look like: giving, giving, giving until I was completely depleted, until I had nothing left.

Even when I started treatment, the idea of taking time away from them—and for something so trivial as a bath—was extremely difficult for me. There was also the added guilt I had about being so ill for so long, not to mention the eighteen months prior to that, when my foot was broken and I needed so much support and assistance from my family. If it wasn't for the need to detox after those treatments, I likely would never have done it. I never would have realized that in loving myself, I would ultimately be a better mom to my children.

Long before the illness, I had been telling myself a story about my responsibilities to my family. Much of it was in reaction to how I was raised and the different mother I was determined to be. Also, after Billy was born, my husband began traveling more for work, and I became the primary parent.

Over time, this became part of the story—only I could do things the "right way." It wasn't Dennis' fault; he just wasn't around as much and didn't know what the boys needed like I did. Now, I was reframing that story because physical healing was my number one priority. I was expanding my comfort zone to include taking time for myself. It was out of necessity, I told myself. I now know Spirit was tricking me, bypassing my resistance to get me into the water.

It was in the bath that I would start to love my body, and see clearly, for the first time, all the ways in which I had not treated it lovingly before. This didn't happen immediately. Each night, I would light some candles, then turn the lights off and sink into the warm water, allowing it to envelop and soothe me. Having only candlelight illuminating my form made it easier to feel the energy of unconditional love without the visual reminder of flaws. When I added meditation, it went from a relaxing ritual to a magical one.

I was new to meditation, having done it only once at one of Sunny's in-person classes. For about eight to ten minutes, she guided us to invoke the blue energy of Archangel Michael. The length is important to mention, because a lot of people think you have to meditate for thirty minutes, an hour, or even longer. This is not true.

We need only to plug into that spot for seconds to feel it. If it takes some practice to get into that space, it is fine. This is not a race, nor is it a time for shaming or pressuring yourself. It is ONLY about sacred, authentic connection.

I was able to drop right in and experience the frequency of expansion, that space without thoughts, for the first time. Again, it was probably easier because my mind wasn't clouded by all the different ways one could and should meditate. There is nothing quite like *knowing nothing*.

With my beginner's mind, there was no expectation, no debate over whether I was doing it "right" or "wrong." I had absolutely no clue where it would lead; I didn't know it would lead anywhere at all. (In fact, you don't "go" anywhere; rather, you sit in the space and allow it to come to you.) I will say that once I had found it and knew how it felt, I didn't keep looking or trying to make it anything else. I could connect very quickly.

It was in this state, with my limbs resting and my mind soft, that class began, with information in the form of downloads or images offering explanations. Some of these explanations were for things I hadn't even realized I was questioning.

This was coming in much differently than the information I had previously been getting—those were little "blinks" of awareness when my mother was around or Morse code messages I had to decipher. It was as if the bath, the water, created an incubator that really intensified and magnified the connection.

It made the veil really thin, so for the first time, I didn't pop right back to my normal timeline but was able to hold the frequency long enough to get those downloads and integrate them. In the bath, there was more time and space. I could allow; I could stay longer in the water to get that information, to understand the two worlds I was inhabiting.

"Wow, I'm really smart!"—something I had always thought when I "just knew" something—was replaced with the realization that this information was coming from somewhere and someone else. I also realized that the signs I had gotten from my mother were not just about the actual messages from her, but about creating just enough of an opening for me to accept this ... and the angels that would soon start coming to me.

One by one, I learned who they were and how they felt. They were teaching me how to discern between different frequencies and energies. In the process, I was also learning what my own energy felt like.

That's when they started showing me, like a movie screen in my mind, certain things I had experienced, and how the energy had remained stuck in my body. It began gently, with things I had witnessed, read about, or experienced as a probation officer, as that would have felt safer at the time.

I recall being shown a man who had been one of my most difficult defendants. I had worked with him for years and spent a great deal of time with him and on his case. There was a lot of really disturbing energy around him, and I had unknowingly absorbed all of that toxicity. As they showed me this, the energy resurfaced, but because I was safe in the bath, I felt into it rather than pushing it down like I had when it was happening.

One night, after connecting to Source energy through my crown, I had an incredibly surreal experience of coming down into my body with a flashlight. I looked around and saw all the trauma I had put in boxes and tucked away on shelves, some for decades, that were now coming up to be felt and released. I also saw all the damage this had done to my body and thought, "Holy shit, what a mess I've made."

It was a moment of taking accountability, and a lot of shame for how the disease had affected how I showed up for my kids. I knew how it felt to grow up with a sick mom and had, unknowingly, given energy to it, thus manifesting the same situation. Along with that shame, however, I had awareness that I was being shown this because I had the power to change it.

I was learning how to transmute energy. I would teach this differently now (more on that later), but I was taught to send it love and Light and visualization. To do this, I had to tap into unconditional love for self, and then open it up to see, experience, and shift it.

Enlightenment 101: To do anything, be it transmuting stuck energy or manifesting what we desire, we must be present in the body. This is when we step into our power.

They also showed me how, whether we are in the body or not, and no matter what is happening to the body, the safety of our soul is *never* in doubt. On the "movie screen" that night was the sexual assault. I saw how my soul had left my body and was up with the angels, even as my physical form and my personality self were being overpowered below.

When we're doing this work, all sorts of uncomfortable feelings will come up—things like shame, guilt, and so on. BUT/AND, we also see from an expanded perspective how these experiences we viewed as traumas were opportunities for growth and expansion. Lower-vibing energies associated with these things are not meant to be held on to, but acknowledged and allowed to flow out, just like the water that goes down when we drain the tub.

While in the bath, I began to learn what it meant to hold my frequency—to stay aligned with a higher state of energy, awareness, and presence, no matter what was happening around me. This is a core part of spiritual embodiment.

Holding your frequency means maintaining your inner light, clarity, and truth—even in the face of fear, doubt, or discomfort. It's about anchoring into who you are at a soul level and choosing not to drop into old patterns or lower vibrations.

Over time, this practice deepened my intuitive connection. I could hear, feel, and trust the guidance more clearly. I later added daily walks in nature, which became another sacred touchpoint for connection and grounding. Eventually, those twice-daily check-ins with Spirit became a steady, ongoing conversation—one I now carry with me through all aspects of my life.

SPILL IN AISLE FOUR

Truth resonates at a certain frequency. You cannot describe it with words; you have to feel it, and once you do, you will never accept anything different.

Over the next several months, the combination of IV treatments and my nightly "lessons" in the bath began chipping away at my despair and making way for some hope. There was definitely physical improvement—I was about eighty percent better—but I knew I was treating symptoms rather than getting to the root cause.

Also, there were still symptoms that remained untouched, especially around my eyes and sinuses. The brain fog and inflammation were there as well. There was this sense of a missing piece, something that would lead to a tipping point, get me over an invisible hurdle. I just had no idea what that something might be.

It wasn't for lack of trying. As mentioned earlier, even before my official diagnosis, I had been told by my mother that it was Lyme. Though I didn't share this with anyone, I'd been tireless in researching the symptoms, possible causes, and anything that could help.

A Google search at that time yielded only the basic facts, "… the disease is named for Lyme, Connecticut, where the first outbreak occurred …" and "it comes from a tick bite …," that kind of simplistic nonsense that told me nothing at all. I had also joined several Lyme groups on social media, and though it was comforting to know I wasn't alone, I hadn't gotten much actionable information.

One night, after coming out of meditation, I saw a social media post from a group I wasn't part of, sharing the science behind Lyme and a dozen coinfections that were often worse than the original.

As soon as I clicked on it, I experienced a feeling that I was on the right track. When I dug deeper, I discovered Steve Beddingfield, who'd had a journey similar to mine and healed himself without the help of Western medicine.

I joined the group, unsure whether I was there for guidance or out of raw desperation and despair. It didn't matter much because as Steve spoke, I was immediately drawn in. I liked that he had a science background and had turned to science for answers. Everything he explained made perfect sense. He also validated everything that had happened to me. Much like the bath, I was being invited to "school"—one with a different curriculum but ultimately about the same thing: peeling off the blinders.

Our healthcare industry, like other systems, is very invested in our compliance. To achieve this, they create a lot of noise (i.e., providing false information and/or withholding it altogether) in the hopes that we will be distracted and confused, and we will believe we need them.

> *The only falsehood we have to worry about is the one that tells us we're powerless. Buying into that is how we give our power away, not just with our health, but in countless ways every day.*

Like most of us, I had the noise turned up to maximum volume. As far back as I could remember, I had gotten up each morning and listened to the mainstream news as I got ready for my day, with no awareness of the frequency I was vibrating to.

My perspective on the media had begun to shift back when I was in law enforcement and reported to news outlets about high-profile cases I was working. It was not uncommon to later see these stories inaccurately conveyed to the public, often through the omission of gender, ethnicity, or criminal charges of those involved.

At the time, I didn't question whether this was intentional or not. Even when I did realize they were "packaging" the information to sell an agenda, I didn't understand the level of manipulation and control that was happening. I had grown up watching *60 Minutes* with my grandfather on Sunday nights. I remember the authoritative voices of the hosts and correspondents, the soothing tick, tick, tick of that famous clock. The perception was that the media were looking out for us, as were the government, the doctors, and the schools.

Collectively, these systems make up the ant farm, and we are conditioned from birth to trust in them unconditionally. They shape our perspective of the world and what we are capable of doing. When we give our trust without awareness, we are blinded to our own truth and, therefore, to the ways to navigate and grow through challenges.

The U.S. medical system is run by pharmaceutical companies, and they market through fear. Every other commercial is some celebrity pushing one drug or another. Like any other media, they are throwing out those energetic fishing lines to anyone who will take them.

The effect is twofold: they give the appearance that illness is inevitable (making it more likely people will manifest it) and that they need allopathic meds to manage it. Notice I said "manage," not "cure." This ensures our enslavement and, since people are living longer, guarantees them countless revenue streams in perpetuity. Doctors also get paid bonuses for administering vaccines (during the pandemic, it was revealed that they were receiving two hundred dollars per injection of the COVID-19 vaccines). Other countries do not have this.

Am I saying no one should use Western medicine? No, nor am I telling you to never get inoculated against some virus. Am I telling you that every allopathic doctor only cares about money? Of course not. What I am saying is that when we realize it's a business, and it has led us to become the sickest nation in the world, we can think critically and make better decisions for ourselves. We will find a Western medicine doctor who also sees past the system to learn about alternatives, provides holistic care, and, most importantly, listens to their patients. We will also spot the disingenuous naturopaths, so-called "healers," and so on.

When I met Steve, I was just starting to realize the enormity of this. I was also still straddling two realities and very much aware that I had reached out to some "cuckoo" on the internet. It made no sense to my logical mind, and yet, I trusted him. From a simple background and extremely humble, Steve devoted hours upon hours sharing and teaching and helping, and he was not charging anyone a cent for his time. I had never experienced anything like that.

All the information I had been so desperately searching for was now coming in faster than I could process it. I learned that the CDC had continued to use a highly ineffective test for Lyme, contributing greatly to false negatives; those negatives were then used to dismiss and gaslight patients who experienced symptoms. My nightmare "Birkenstocks doc" was their creation. (The CDC's lack of accountability and incompetence would later be borne out in this *Forbes*[3] article comparing the agency's failures regarding

---

[3] Mary Beth Pfeiffer, "Lessons from Lyme Disease: Six Reasons the CDC's Covid-19 Failure Was Predictable," Forbes, March 13, 2020, https://www.forbes.com/sites/marybethpfeiffer/2020/03/13/lessons-from-lyme-disease-six-reasons-the-cdcs-covid-19-failure-was-predictable/.

COVID with its handling of Lyme. But that revelation was still a few years in the future.)

Steve also talked about the body and toxins in our environment in everything we consume—from what we eat, drink, and smoke to the waves that come off our devices. They disrupt the body's natural state, which is one of balance and health, and its ability to recalibrate and heal itself.

Specifically, he focused on parasites and fungi such as the Aspergillus species,[4] which cause widespread and often undiagnosed infections in both people and animals. These fungal infections are resistant to drugs and potentially deadly, especially for those with compromised immune systems.

As for the parasites, they not only cause diseases, but they also eat our bones and therefore affect our structural systems. Every autoimmune disease is caused by parasites, as are cancer and mental health conditions. I broke my foot three times because of the bone demineralization resulting from parasites.

Again, every word he spoke rang with truth.

Our bodies are made up of mostly water, anywhere from sixty to eighty percent. When we come into contact with heavy metals and parasites—via our food, kisses from a pet, or countless other ways—the body becomes a dirty aquarium.

Another analogy is that of an ice glacier. There are different microorganisms present, and as the glacier melts, they enter our environment. Individual factors, such as the acidity in one's body, how much movement they get, diet (i.e., parasites love sugar), their

---

[4] Eric Ralls, "Fungus that can 'eat you from the inside out' is spreading around the world," earth.com, N.D. https://www.earth.com/news/deadly-fungus-aspergillus-that-can-eat-you-from-the-inside-out-is-quietly-spreading-around-the-world/?fbclid=IwQ0xDSwL P7e9leHRuA2FlbQIxMQABHsHH5AdMex2ulyvuzYfHheHsni45orkqoL5AUbbnU-IQS3QJe91flndUETcH_aem_D_viomgTmSPvmbDrQun7Zg

emotions, and, of course, the frequency at which they're vibrating, all play a huge role.

My "aquarium" was filled with a green sludge you couldn't even see through—a combination of the Lyme, the effects of the stem cell surgery, and all the energy from painful experiences that had been stuck in my body. These toxins and decay would have to be cleared from my tissues, one layer at a time.

Then Steve mentioned how something called fenbendazole (FenBen), an antiparasitic used to treat animals, helps to heal the layers of toxicity. (This was what he had taken to heal himself.) Study after study has shown that FenBen cures autoimmune stuff and cancer and helps with just about everything else.

Despite this, and the fact that many people in other countries take it, FenBen is approved in the U.S. only for animal consumption. Our doctors are not even taught about it. He also talked about a medication made from red reishi mushrooms and the benefits of iodine.

After several conversations with Steve, in which he answered every one of my questions, I ordered FenBen from overseas. That's the thing about being close to death—you tend to stop giving a shit about some government agency's approval, or lack thereof. I had been playing the game their way long enough because I didn't know what else to do; now that I had been given another option, I was going to take it.

When you see how these systems work, you are no longer deterred by their smokescreens or barriers. You understand that if you're open to seeing breadcrumbs and acting on them, you will be guided every step of the way.

To say that this stuff was absolutely disgusting is an understate-
ment. Back then, FenBen didn't come in pill form, likely because the
goats and horses who normally took it preferred a paste; the "bitter
apple" flavor, so appealing to our four-legged friends, was also hard
to deal with. But, in less than two weeks, I experienced noticeable

improvement, with the brain fog that had plagued me clearing up almost immediately.

This was unbelievable (I even wondered if I was experiencing a placebo effect because I wanted it to work so badly), and yet somehow I had this feeling of inevitability about it. Indeed, everything had fallen into place in the order it needed to. Had I found Steve first, I would have been too sick to take the medicines he recommended. I had to have that year of infusions with the naturopath first. Healing is natural, but it takes energy. The IVs "shocked my system," like shocking a pool with chemicals to get rid of the algae that forms on top. This got me sixty percent of the way there, so my immune system was strong enough to start treating the parasites.

For a while, I continued to go to the naturopath for infusions, which, along with the FenBen, created the perfect healing cocktail for my body. I also told no one, including the naturopath and my husband, about what I was doing.

In 2017, nobody was talking about what parasites do to the body; certainly, it was not in the mainstream. Someone taking goat paste would have to be crazy. As it turned out, being threatened with a mental institution was valuable training for me. I knew I wasn't crazy; I knew there were medical professionals willing to gaslight me; I knew I wasn't going to let them do it.

That said, I was also no fool, which is why I played things so close to the vest. Dennis wouldn't learn of it for at least six months, when the results were more apparent. In other words, until I had clear evidence of my sanity.

Often, those considered "crazy" are simply those who trust their inner knowing and Spirit about what they hear and see in the physical. I would still be considered crazy if I hadn't gotten better.

One such piece of evidence presented itself during a trip to the supermarket with Kristi, my former law enforcement partner. Though we hadn't worked together in more than fifteen years, we had remained best friends, continuing to grow together and support each other.

I think this is in part because our relationship was never about going out and drinking and meeting guys. Sure, we could always go for a beer after work, but we had a different kind of foundation. It's like having a sibling without all the shared childhood trauma, though we surely had trauma-bonded over what we had witnessed in a decade at the department.

Kristi was also one of the few people who stood by me one hundred percent when I was sick. I recall her going with me to the Birkenstocks doc and asking her point-blank, "So, there's *nothing* you can do?" The doctor's response: an equally point-blank, "No," followed by an inference that I needed mental health treatment. Kristi couldn't fathom this; she had witnessed my decline; she knew I was dying; and she was advocating for me.

On this particular day, she had taken me to an appointment with another doctor (I was doing much better but still had a ways to go), then we stopped to pick up some groceries. It was then that my hearing, which I had lost in one ear over a year earlier, suddenly came back.

When I first heard the voice over the PA system in my "bad" ear, I didn't believe it. I turned to Kristi and asked, "What did they just say?" and she confirmed what I thought the voice had said. The words "spill in aisle four" will forever be among the most beautiful words I've ever heard.

This journey is never happening on just one level. We cannot see all the pieces; however, when we do the work to release the denser energies like shame and unworthiness and when we stop trying to control and start surrendering and trusting Spirit and Higher Self, we make space for miracles to come in.

Once I started taking FenBen, I knew I was cured—even before my hearing returned and years before my hair grew back. Spirit confirmed this, adding that my physical healing would be a five-year process. My initial reaction: Five years?! Can I do this for five years? But when I thought about the alternative and began to take stock of the progress I had already made, I decided that, yes, I most certainly could do it. Also, it did get easier. I was feeling better and better; I was able to gradually, with plenty of work, start doing things I did before my illness and much more.

This helped me to keep believing, even when the final piece in my physical healing—the regrowth of my hair—hadn't happened yet. When that did occur in 2023, seven years into my journey, it was because I had learned the lesson to love myself, with or without the beauty queen's golden curls, and my external reflected that inner vibration back to me.

I even came to accept that I would always have to manage and maintain my "aquarium." I now have a team of half a dozen different naturopaths who specialize in different modalities, from energy to hormones to frequency healing. I also have a wonderful team of integrative MDs who chose to create a practice focusing on the whole body and patient needs.

The fact is, we are in physical bodies, living on this planet where, again, we are constantly coming into contact with parasites. We treat our animals with antiparasitic medicine, and as we are mammals too, it only makes sense that we would do the same for ourselves. Other countries do this, while the U.S. doesn't even acknowledge it. After all, treating parasites is far cheaper than treating all the illnesses they cause, to the tune of billions of dollars a year.

Most people can manage this and be asymptomatic on low levels of antiparasitic treatment and through lifestyle choices. My case was extreme because of the stem cell surgery that activated all the viruses.

Equally important, my vibration was so low that I unconsciously called in energies matching that frequency. If I hadn't gotten so sick, I never would have delved deeper to learn about things like frequency; I would have taken a pill and been done with it.

This is what I needed energetically to wake up.

"I'M FROM *WHERE?*"

A spiritual awakening can be an extremely uncomfortable and painful space to be in if we are unaware and don't have support. On the one hand, we can feel ourselves expanding, which is exciting and sparks curiosity to see what else is there for us; on the other, we feel caught between a rock and a hard place—afraid of falling into the unknown and afraid of sliding backward.

That's where I was in 2017—another pivotal year, but one very different from 2014. Then, everything was falling apart; now, things were on an upward trajectory, but a very tentative one.

I was about a year into feeling better, but still quite ill and terrified of getting worse again. I was also getting bombarded with information, signs, and synchronicities, which I was opening to but didn't fully trust. I was still looking for validation of that information, as well as answers about my health, my purpose, and just about everything else, outside myself.

The unknown is where the miracles happen. Getting there requires our surrender of the known, and that's where the fear comes in. Understand that what feels like falling is actually progress. We may plateau for a while; we may choose to stay in that space, and that is okay. But there is no going back. Once we know, we cannot "unknow." Once we reach a certain level of awareness, it becomes a part of us.

I made an appointment for a reading with Daniel, a well-known intuitive from Maui, whom I had been guided to. Up to that point, my only frame of reference for such things was a reading I'd gotten from Sunny after my mom passed. I had also, as mentioned, gotten several direct messages from Mom and noticed that they often arrived in response to my request for support.

As a result of Sunny's reading and the repeated and undeniable signs I received, I had started to believe that there was a two-way communication going on, that Mom was not just around but actively supporting me. My comfort level had expanded to this point (which was no small thing considering where I'd started), so that was the kind of connection I was looking for when I booked this reading. I expected to hear things like, "Your mom is here and she wants you to know that you're going to be fine. Your health will not regress again," and so on.

Spirit had a very different idea.

Recently, I played the recording of the reading. I hadn't listened to Daniel's messages since that day, and I wanted to make sure I correctly recounted them in the book. But what struck me most was how different *my* voice sounded—faint, hesitant, doubting.

In my defense, how was I supposed to react when, for the first several minutes, the guy said nothing in any human language, but instead emitted a series of unintelligible, high-pitched sounds? Every now and then, he would pause, sometimes for what seemed like a full minute or more; then, just when I was wondering whether I should say something, he would start again. No explanation, just those beep-beeps and screechy sounds. Even on the recording, I could "hear" my thought of *WTF!?* hanging in the air between us.

"You came in with a lot of multidimensional energy," he said finally, "and you have to learn how to ground it."

It didn't matter that he was, well, *using words*, because I had no idea what they meant. He explained that my soul had originally taken form in Andromeda, a realm far beyond Earth, in a high-frequency system where embodiment is rare and light is the primary language. This gave me pause, because I had heard the word "Andromeda" once before, from my higher self during a meditation.

Yes, Daniel continued, I had lived lifetimes on Earth before, as well as in other cosmic realms like Sirius B and beyond, but a part of my soul still carried the frequency of that original place. A place where physicality wasn't the norm—where things were fluid, expansive, and far less dense than here.

In the years since that reading, I have heard of people who feel like they are "not from around here"—here, meaning this planet. Most have felt from a very early age that they don't belong on Earth. They wonder what they are doing here and not in a life purpose kind of way. They feel weird and out of step with humans, including those considered their nearest and dearest. They express a desire to "go home" and see their "real" or "star" family.

All of this sounded, for lack of a better word, completely "alien" to me. My intention when scheduling that reading had nothing to do with learning about spirituality, and certainly not to learn what *galaxy* I was from.

I was there for answers about my third-dimensional life, about my physical healing, which was still my number one focus. I was working with Steve and seeing results, but I wanted to know if there was something more I could be doing to expedite that healing. I wanted my hair to grow back, for crying out loud! Instead, I was hearing stuff that sounded batshit crazy … BUT/AND, there was also that slight opening in my armor; I had just enough curiosity and hope to stay on the call.

So, I waited, playing along, letting everything go in one ear and out the other. Then, once the strange noises and the galactic stuff were over, I asked the questions that were still haunting my every day: "Am I going to get sicker again? Are my husband and kids okay?" At that time, I not only still believed I was dying, but I was also terrified that I was putting my family at risk.

By this point, I had learned a lot from Steve's community and my own intuitive hits about Lyme; however, I'd also gotten enough conflicting information, particularly on how contagious it is. It seemed the only thing everyone could agree on was that it passed from mother to unborn child through the placenta. Some sources said it was sexually transmitted; others said there was "no credible evidence" of this. I didn't know what to believe.

Again, what I needed from the intuitive that day was confirmation that we would all be okay. Instead, he started telling me things that sounded just as weird as the other stuff—i.e., how I could shift my health by *breathing* a certain way. He also said I should visualize being well and some other things too. I had never heard of things like breathwork; what's more, it didn't resonate *at all*.

I remember thinking snarkily, *Oh, wow! Who knew I just had to breathe and "think my way" into being better? Why didn't I think of that?!* It sounded ridiculous and a complete waste of my time. And if that wasn't enough, as he closed the reading, he thanked me for stepping forward and shining light. He then added that I would be known as a "consciousness pioneer" and would help many.

What. The. Actual. Fuck.

It is amazing how differently those words land now. All those "crazy" things he talked about are things I do all the time. That is how I move energy! I teach about consciousness!

He was both "predicting" the future and witnessing an aspect of me I had yet to recognize and bring to the fore. At the time, it was simply not in alignment with me. I wasn't there yet, and in fact, I shut down everything he said for about two more years.

That is not self-judgment, but self-awareness. What matters is that I took the leap to make the appointment, stay on the call, and keep the recording. That reading taught me a very valuable lesson about our level of awareness and expectations based on that level of awareness. What sounds like utter bullshit when we are in one space is received as golden nuggets of wisdom when we are in another. How do we get there? By taking baby steps.

Spirit is always planting seeds, always placing the breadcrumbs in our path. The importance of following the breadcrumbs, especially when we feel like we are flying blind, cannot be overstated. Keeping some account of our journey is also valuable, for it is tangible evidence of how far we have already come.

These days, I see the information the intuitive conveyed to me, and the way in which he conveyed it, very differently. This is because I have gone through the process of learning to trust the information I receive, even though it looks different from what I expect or what others may receive.

For example, I sense and get messages from crossed-over loved ones, but I don't necessarily give people "mediumship readings" in the traditional sense. I am much better at translating the information coming down and communicating it with those who need to hear it. This feels fucking great, but I am not attached to the message in any way. It's simply energy, moving through me.

I have since realized that during my awakening, I did tap into my multidimensional self. My Higher Self told me that I was from a star system I had never heard of. I had channeled sessions revealing that I'd spent numerous lifetimes in other systems.

I've also had my own experiences to validate what I've been told. I've seen myself in different star systems—at an energy school in a different dimension, at Atlantis. I resonate with this now; I own it.

What I do not resonate with is, "I'm a starseed. I am chosen."

We are *all* made of stars. We are all a divine spark of consciousness connected to Source. For the first forty-five years of this life, my level of awareness was in the third dimension, and then I tapped into a higher awareness. Period. Everyone can do the same. In fact, everyone is doing it already. We are collectively going through a massive ascension period, just as the Earth is. When we're not aware of this, it can look like everything is falling apart, which makes us feel bat-shit crazy.

The important takeaway here is that it's all energy. When we understand this, tapping into multidimensional energies does not seem all that outlandish; in fact, it makes perfect sense. We can still be part of this earthly "ant farm," and we can also tap into this. The higher your vibration, the better it feels. It thus becomes a question of where you want to spend your energy.

What do these baby steps look like? For me, it was being willing to see the naturopath and then Steve, when all my previous "logical" beliefs would have told me it was nonsense. It was opening up to talking to Sunny, who started me on the path of learning about energy. It was starting to meditate, and leaning into the feeling that "there is more for me," which led to learning about Reiki and the realization that my soul *remembered* not only how to do it, but that gemstones amplify the healing. I learned about the power of my emotions and the need to express them, and how to move the energy through breathwork. Through it all, it has been about maintaining the momentum, having accountability, and taking inspired action. It was every little piece.

It was *not* waking up one day and deciding I was going to do yoga and become a vegetarian. I am not judging these things. What I am saying is that it is all about what *you are called to do*, not what you heard someone else did or read in a book or saw on a YouTube video.

How do we know what we are being called to do? First, by turning down the noise. We are bombarded by talking heads, all clamoring to instruct us how things are, what they should be, how we need to act and think, and what we need to say to make it so. They do not have the answers. Now, can you hear a piece of data, acknowledge it as having a vibration of truth, and follow the breadcrumb? Yes! But the actual guidance is coming from within—always.

Second, we begin to connect and build a relationship with Spirit and our Higher Self. They know our intention for our life, and when we are tapped in, we gain access to the downloads that guide us to the next step.

My intention is to become as spiritually evolved as I can in this lifetime. I am committed to doing the work to get me there. Now that I have this relationship with Higher Self and Spirit, they help me meet my goals by giving me growth opportunities.

At first, seeing these opportunities as such (as opposed to merely shitty situations) and taking action was incredibly hard work; it was getting up every time I fell. What I now realize is that "hard work" was my frame of reference at the time. It had been hard before, so it would continue to be hard, right? Only if we continue to hold this frame of awareness. Once I was tapped in and becoming a creator, I knew I was never alone. There were still challenges, sure, but it never felt that hard again. Once I passed each threshold, I never slid back to where I was before.

Neither will you.

Spirit has, on numerous occasions, "tricked" me into taking the steps. What I mean is that they give me nudges, telling me to do this or that, knowing that my "personality" self will fill in what I think is the purpose.

More often than not, that purpose is much more expanded and much more uncomfortable than I contemplated. This book is a perfect example. What began as a nudge to share my story with the world is also an opportunity to further embody the energy through the writing process.

Can you recall a time when Spirit tricked you? A time you had an inexplicable feeling to do something, or a nudge for what you thought was a particular reason, only to realize later it had a much grander purpose or was a breadcrumb on the path?

This energy can move through everyone the same way—including you. If you are doubting this and saying, "Me, no way! I'm not that special," or thinking that I sound batshit crazy and all you wanted when you picked up this book was to manifest a new car, go back and reread what I wrote about my galactic reading.

I thought he was full of it, and that what he said, if it even existed, had nothing to do with me.

After the reading, I googled consciousness, because I had no idea what that meant!

I followed the breadcrumbs anyway. I took baby steps, even when I didn't know what I was doing. Now I look back and remember—ahh, yes, this step led to this one and so on.

I am now living in the space he spoke of.

THE PORTAL

Daily meditation changed everything for me. Period. It was beautiful. It was relaxing. It was expansive. *I was expansive.* It was so much of all these things that after several months, I thought that was it. I thought I had "arrived."

"Ha, ha," said Spirit. "Not quite."

We never arrive. At first, this may seem scary, exhausting, and even infuriating. This is a natural reaction when we are used to struggling through third-dimensional challenges from a third-dimensional perspective.

The third dimension, or 3D, refers to the level of consciousness where most of us begin our human experience—where we view life through the lens of duality, separation, fear, and survival. It's the realm of right and wrong, success and failure, good and bad. In this space, we tend to believe that fulfillment lies somewhere outside of us—that if we can just "get there," then we'll finally be okay.

We want to clear the hurdle; we want to start coasting. We want to get there, whatever that means. But as our awareness increases, we begin to see the beauty in the never-ending journey. We understand that "never arriving" simply means we are limitless, capable of expanding beyond the great imaginings of the human mind. We are also able to see challenges as

growth opportunities and move through them with far more
ease, grace, light, and joy.

It's important to mention that while my body was relaxing in the tub, I was also doing a lot of work. What did the work look like? It was learning how to be still and quiet and to enjoy it, which was not always easy after a lifetime of noise.

I made a ritual out of it, with Epsom salts, crystals, incense, and candles. I set intentions. Sometimes I listened to chanting or music. Deva Premal, who sings in Sanskrit, was a favorite. Sanskrit, the first recorded human language, has a resonance of truth that I could feel even though I didn't understand the words. It's important to note that in the beginning I did a few more guided meditations as I learned to trust my own guidance and journey. Remember, I am all about baby steps, and this is an important one if you're new to meditation or have found it challenging.

There was never any TV or podcasts in the bath.

Like most things in life, meditation is not going to look like what we think it will. People meditate for different reasons, similar to yoga and breathwork. For some, it's to improve their physical health, such as reducing stress and lowering blood pressure, and it definitely does that pretty quickly. This is more of a third-dimensional approach, and it's all great and healthy and perfect. It will also lead to spiritual expansion for those who are open to it.

However, if you're meditating with the intention of connecting deeply with Spirit and manifesting things into your life, you may find yourself feeling like nothing is happening, that you're wasting your time.

First, it can take a while to connect. Second, many of us have the impression that once we get there, the energy will come right through, and we are going to get all the answers in that session. This also points to a third-dimensional approach, but because the desire is different, it's going to feel frustrating.

No matter how it may seem, there is a lot of development going on energetically, behind the scenes. Are there amazing moments, with mind-blowing downloads and breakthroughs and all of that? Sure. But, more often than not, that meditation is a space to set your intention and hang out with Spirit. Then Spirit gets to work and begins dropping in the breadcrumbs. We can choose to follow them, or not. That said, it usually doesn't happen during the meditation session; they drift into our everyday life and can be disguised if we're not present, open, and connected.

If what you intended has not shown up yet, that's telling you that you still have to get out of your way and release the expectation of how it's going to show up. Holding tight to the idea of one moment when you suddenly hear harps and become enlightened will affect your experience, and certainly the pacing of it.

Again, my lack of "book knowledge" on this stuff served me well. I had no spiritual dogma or other people's experiences floating around in my head, thus I had little to no expectation. I just found myself really looking forward to the solitude and stillness, this space where all of my senses were engaged.

As I mentioned earlier, it was in this space that I learned to love myself, including my body. And I was learning to love it, not in spite of my illness but because of it. This is a huge piece, because I had been battling my body in one form or another since I was three years old.

Once I got sick, this became even more acute because I felt betrayed by and imprisoned in this physical vessel. Now I was offering it love and appreciation, even those less-than-perfect areas like my broken foot, my "mother pouch," cellulite, and lack of hair, lashes, and eyebrows. I was doing this even though—and this is important—I didn't believe it.

I felt like I was pretending.

I felt like I was making stuff up.

It was hard as hell, but I did it anyway.

I also sincerely *wanted* to believe it, and that's what made the difference.

Mirror work became a powerful tool for me during this time. It's the practice of standing in front of a mirror and, instead of picking apart your reflection or zeroing in on what you think is wrong, you begin to look at yourself with compassion. You speak to yourself with kindness. You try to see through the eyes of love.

I had never done that before. Honestly, most of us haven't. We're so conditioned to be critical—trained from an early age by family, media, relationships, and culture to judge ourselves against impossible standards. We internalize those messages so deeply that we don't even realize how harsh we've become with ourselves.

But when I began showing up to the mirror with intention—even if it felt awkward or fake at first—something in me started to soften.

> *A lot of us get in our head; we want to see how this is all going to look, and we shame ourselves for not being able to figure it out. That's not our job; nor do we have to believe everything hook, line, and sinker.*
>
> *Our job is to open up the energy. The desire for change shifts the energy. It opens the door. It changes the timeline. It allows Spirit—who does know everything—to come in and do Its magic.*

In the meantime, my classes with Spirit continued. Each night, I would settle in the bath, tap in, and the lesson would begin. Sometimes, I was given information about this life—about things that had happened or had not yet happened, or the way the systems around us work.

Sometimes, I was shown other lives, not all of them on this planet, in which I was very experienced in working with and transmuting energy. In one life, I was living in Atlantis, attending an energy school similar to Hogwarts.

Again, this was always work; it required the energy and presence to be able to hold that frequency. I didn't understand what I was doing or why it was hard, just that it took concentration to stay in there.

There were plenty of times when I was like, "Okay, I'm going to go meditate and chill out," and, well, that's how Spirit gets you there. I also didn't yet understand that the water was some kind of incubator, which intensified the experience.

Spirit was reminding me that this was not my first rodeo, and these classes were not so much about learning as they were about remembering. Of course, this was a stretch for me at the time, so my teachers provided examples that were hard to dispute.

The first incident happened on the night Spirit showed me a long-time offender who had taken his life. After finishing my meditation, I got out of the tub, drained it, and headed into the separate shower. I often used bentonite clay in my baths—it's great for detoxing, but thick and hard to rinse off, so the shower helped wash it away.

As I stepped under the warm stream of water, I didn't give a second thought to the candle still flickering nearby. It was set beside the tub, close, but not touching, a decorative faux tree I'd had for years.

Then I got a sudden, unmistakable nudge to look around the corner.

When I did, I saw the tree fully engulfed in flames.

I screamed for my husband. Thankfully, the tub was still draining, so I had a full reservoir of water to throw on it and smother the fire before it could spread.

Later, I kept wondering: *How the hell did that happen?* The candle wasn't directly touching the tree. I'd taken countless baths like this before with candles nearby—same setup, no issue. But this time was different. This time, there had been a *release*.

I asked Sunny what the hell had just happened, expecting something like, "Be more careful with candles." Instead, she burst out laughing.

She knew exactly what had happened. The fire was a manifestation of the intensity of energy that had just been moved and transmuted during that session—specifically the heavy, dense vibration connected to the suicide.

The moment I shifted it, that energy had to go somewhere, and because the space was already charged—the water acting like an amplifier, the candle holding flame, the proximity of organic matter—the release became physical.

Fire, like water, is a cleanser. In this case, it was both messenger and mirror. A dramatic one, yes, but unmistakable.

What I hadn't understood yet was that these baths weren't just relaxing rituals. They were alchemical chambers. The water amplified my sensitivity. The candle, the clay, the very air in the room—they were part of the container. And when Spirit said, *This isn't your first rodeo*, they weren't kidding. This wasn't just learning, it was remembering. And sometimes … the remembering gets loud.

Not two weeks later, I was in the bath working on another lesson. It had to do with a situation with Billy, more specifically, my perspective on the situation. He was going through a very difficult time emotionally, and I was working on witnessing his emotions without taking them all on. I was aware of my sense of responsibility for the way he was feeling.

Today, I know that I am not responsible—that no one is responsible—for how another feels, whether it's a complete stranger or a child. Back then, it was a very different story. I had guilt, and I was projecting. I was failing to see that he is a sovereign being, and this was his life journey. All I could think was, *He had a sick mom, and now he's going through this. And it's all because of me.* I was spiraling into victimhood, where I had been so many times before.

These were precisely the kinds of feelings I would normally push down, put in the trauma box. Now, because I was ready to release what no longer served, I was feeling all of it. In fact, I was sitting in it, as if it were debris in the water.

Emotions are "energy in motion," or at least that's what they are supposed to be. When we push our emotions away, we are burying the energy, and that's what makes us sick and stuck.

When we stop running and allow ourselves to feel them, that energy moves through and out of us and back into Mother Earth, where it is transmuted. Then we can take our power back and do something. This is the choice point, a fork in the road. We must choose not to go back to the way we've always done things and instead lean into the new, lean into our pain and discomfort. And—yay!—that night, I was doing it! I was leaning into ...

That's when the fire alarm and sprinkler system went off.

WTAF?!

We were having a flood in our casita, which is located on the other side of the master bedroom, where I was. This time, I quickly realized what was happening. Water is a symbol of emotion, and I was allowing the energy of my emotions to move. This was great validation of my power, not to mention more tangible evidence that I was putting Spirit's lessons into practice.

These experiences seemed to be building upon each other, step by step. I had no idea where they were leading, or how huge the shift was going to be.

The portal opened on an otherwise normal night, during an otherwise regular bath meditation. I might have been holding my cintamani jewel for the first time, but I truly can't recall. I just know that, as usual, I tapped in, got aligned, grounded, and centered in that space. Suddenly, in my mind's eye, I saw a circle with smoke around it; then, in the middle of the circle, a door appeared.

Immediately, fear dropped in, and I backed out.

Definitely a what-the-fuck moment.

Two things to note about this: First, my reaction was not a conscious response, but my ego, which was still very much present at that time, stepping in. Second, I learned in this moment that I have control. It wasn't like doors were just going to start opening and I was going to fall through them and end up, like, wherever. This was going to happen on my timeline and according to what I was comfortable with.

As soon as I backed out, I wished I hadn't. I also had awareness that I was judging myself about it.

Why did I just do that? I wanna go through the door!

Then I heard Spirit say, "We didn't want to scare you. If you'd like us to come back, we need your invitation."

With Spirit, it's *never* a doomsday message. It's never, "You need to do this right now or you've missed your shot." There is never any judgment.

It is always about choice.

As soon as I heard, "We didn't want to scare you," I started backpedaling and bargaining.

"Wait! You didn't scare me! Come back!"

I wondered if maybe the portal would immediately open again. It didn't. Instead, I got the chance to really sit with the experience and my reaction to it. Did I trust my Divine guidance? Did I trust the process? How was I really feeling?

I was sure of only one thing: I didn't want to open the door if I was experiencing any kind of fear. Why? Because I had unknowingly and unconsciously danced with low-vibrating frequencies during the illness. I felt it, but because I didn't have awareness and knew nothing about energy, I thought it was mine. I didn't realize that I was simply vibrating at the same frequency.

Another way of saying this: I was concerned my fear could very well bring about a self-fulfilling prophecy. If I indeed had a say in where this path was leading me, it was not back to that space.

In everything we go through, there are kernels of valuable information we can use to propel ourselves forward. To get to it, we sift through and shift our emotions.

I didn't have to wait long—a week or less—before the portal opened again. This time, the visual that came to me was different. Visualization is a very important aspect of creation. What I am going to describe was my visual during that particular bath. The goal here is not for you to emulate my experience, but allow your own visualization, one that feels right and organic for you, knowing that it will be exactly what you need in that moment.

It was daytime, and I was outside, in a lagoon. The water was so clear I could see right through it, and lush greenery surrounded me. I could feel the warmth of the sun on my skin, I could hear the birds singing; I could even smell the water. I was lying on my back, looking up, and I could see mountains. It was as idyllic as a Disney movie.

What I came to understand later was that this was my "safe bubble." It's very interesting because personality/ego Brandi is scared of the water, especially when it's deep. There are fish in there, which I am very afraid of, and God knows what else. But this water was so incredibly clear that I felt safe, even cocooned, just like the bath itself.

It was in this space of being completely safe and protected that I quite accidentally bumped into my Higher Self.

Later, when I retraced my steps to this point, I began to see the incredibly intricate Divine orchestration that is happening all the time.

It was when the doctors I had believed were there to help me were not.

It was when my husband did not speak up for me, but told everybody I was looking for attention.

It was when my entire life—my health, my marriage—was crumbling.

All of this was happening for me; it was bringing down the old so something new, something of a higher frequency, could be built in its place.

I cannot emphasize it enough that THIS WAS NOT HOW IT FELT AT THE TIME. It felt like a battle for my soul, with no idea who was going to win. For sure, my ego had wanted to check out. I had wanted to die. Between the emotional pain and the illness of my body, I didn't see another way out. I felt I lacked the strength to deal with everything alone.

Instead, my choice to surrender activated my inner knowing, and a resilience started to rise. I had to choose to reach for the light. When I did, I realized I had never been alone, not really, not for a minute.

I could have made a very different decision. Had I done so, my life as Brandi would have ended, but my Higher Self, my soul, would still be safe. The path would have looked different, but my soul would have gotten where it was going.

YOU'RE THE ONE
YOU'VE BEEN WAITING FOR

Most of my learnings about an experience came long after the physical piece was resolved. Much dropped in during the writing of this book, as the process of excavating my life for the purpose of helping others led to more transmutation of energies I was still carrying around.

Indeed, I had often believed I had squeezed every drop of wisdom from something, only for my Higher Self and Spirit to come through with another nuance, another layer of the message.

For example, I vividly recall being in meditation and hearing, "You are a bridge." My first reaction: WTF?! I had been having all these new and often strange experiences, and asking what they meant. I wanted to know who, and what, I was.

At that point in my development, "an angel" would have sounded good, but "a bridge"? Again, WTF?! For years, I thought it meant I was the bridge between the ant farm and multidimensional realities—that's what made sense to me at the time.

Through consistent work and as my understanding of concepts like ascension and enlightenment has expanded and evolved, I have come to see this physicality and my role in it very differently. My expedited journey prepared me to help others on theirs. This doesn't make me "chosen," but someone who *has chosen* this as my path for this lifetime.

Our planet, and everything on it, is stepping into a period of expanded consciousness. You may have heard this described as the "New Earth." This is not a place outside of ourselves, a place we have to seek or travel to or construct. We are birthing it, right now, from within our heart center, from within our physical bodies. It embodies what is often referred to as the "Christ consciousness."

I am a bridge between the old world and this new world. My work is not vertical, but horizontal. I'm not a bridge "up," but a bridge "through." When I look at my personal journey through this lens, it is glaringly obvious, in the best possible way, how I was being prepared to serve.

Let me explain.

When we're in the thick of a physical event, be it a sickness, the loss of a person or beloved pet, or some other challenge that threatens our stability in this world, it can be difficult (if not impossible) to see ourselves on the other side.

It feels like we're walking in wet cement with blinders and earplugs on. We don't know where we're going to end up or what that will look like. We are waiting for someone or something to save us—or at least give us information.

Am I going to die? Or, perhaps worse, be sick the rest of my life? Am I going to be alone? Lose my kids? Be locked up for being crazy? Am I destined to end up like my mother?

These are all questions that went through my mind, consciously and subconsciously, for years. As I have mentioned, my physical reality was very much one of pain, isolation, and, above all, cluelessness about where it would all lead.

Often, I was convinced it would end with me leaving this life altogether. No one was more shocked than I when, not only did I live and become well, but a beauty within me had been growing in the darkness, just waiting to spring forward.

It was waiting for me to allow it to emerge.

In many ways, the loss of my hair is the most illustrative of my journey and what I teach today. It was one of the most physically and emotionally painful aspects of my healing. It was also one of the most prolonged, lasting seven years.

Our hair is both a symbol of beauty and our personal style. When we're younger, we dye it for fun; as we age, we dye it to cover the gray. We cut it and grow it according to, or in rebellion against, mainstream fashion. It is the perfect representation of our personality self, of who we think we are. When it is gone, that self-image goes with it.

If you have stuck with me to this point, you might have an idea of what I am about to say: the hair loss (and the loss of that aspect of self) would also lead to a massive spiritual expansion.

The awakening and the illness were happening at the same time—a chicken-or-the-egg situation, for sure. Yes, I had manifested the infection that led to the hair loss, and, yes, the hair loss was giving me an opportunity to expand beyond my previous notions of self. All of this was guided by my Higher Self.

I didn't see it that way at the time, at all. *I didn't know what a Higher Self was.* All I knew was devastation and terror. How much worse could this possibly get?

My hair had actually been thinning for a long time, likely the early signs of inflammation in my body. This was different. I have written about the area at the crown becoming "indented" or "mushy" and so hot and tender it was as if someone had taken a cigarette lighter to my skin. My husband's reaction to that and the feeling that I had been abandoned by him were just one piece of the puzzle.

At the same time, I was also losing my sense of self, especially when the hair around that area began to fall out. The panic around this was intense and, at times, all-consuming. Remember, I also didn't have an answer as to why this was happening. I was not even believed when I told doctors it was happening.

For a couple of weeks, I covered the bald spot on the top of my head with bandanas and hats. I was, at least when around others, able to pretend that I was normal, that my entire life wasn't falling apart. I might have continued this forever, had I not continued to lose my hair at an alarming rate.

Every time a clump broke free from my scalp, I would feel it going down my back, igniting fear and worry in its path. Every time I looked in the mirror, and certainly every time I brushed my hair, those emotions flared.

I had no knowledge of energy or the need to shift those emotions, but I knew I had to do something, for the sake of my mental health, to stop this from happening. I cut my hair very short, well aware that it was just a matter of time before the rest of it was removed. When my hairstylist shaved my head, I felt a surreal combination of horror, loss, and relief. At least I was used to covering my head, which made it easier.

Next stop: the wig store. *Wigs would help me feel normal,* I thought; some were made with real hair and really beautiful. No one would ever guess I was no longer me. They did look great; the problem was, I hated the way they made me feel. The crown area was still so sensitive that anything touching it felt like too much, like when you have a really bad sunburn and even a sheet on it is unbearable.

Just as bad as the physical sensation was the feeling that I was trying to be someone I wasn't. Yet, I continued to wear them. I didn't want to embarrass my husband and sons, nor did I want that attention on me. I didn't want to walk into a restaurant or a store and have people stare at me, pitying me, thinking, *Oh God, that woman is sick. Wonder what's wrong with her?*

After a month of wearing the wig full-time, I struck a balance, putting it on when I went to pick up Billy from school or was otherwise out in public, and leaving it off when around the house.

I also, when at home and wigless, avoided mirrors as much as possible. It wasn't just that I didn't like the way I looked, though that was certainly a big part of it. *I didn't recognize myself.* Imagine looking in the mirror and seeing someone who bears no resemblance to how you feel inside. That was how I felt, like I was staring at a complete stranger.

The child beauty queen, the popular party girl, the tough and competent law enforcement officer, and all the other things that had made Brandi, Brandi, had been erased, leaving this broken-looking person in her place.

Now, in addition to the physical pain and the fear, I was mourning myself as well. In truth, I wasn't losing anything. I was expanding beyond. Did I have any idea this was happening? NO. I just thought it was the illness, stealing everything from me.

I had no idea that the stranger in the mirror was presenting me with an incredible opportunity.

In the last chapter, I talked about mirror work, where you look at your reflection and make positive statements to yourself, such as "I love you" and "You are beautiful."

It is a highly powerful tool of manifestation, and one I wholeheartedly recommend. That said, I was facing two significant challenges in the beginning: I did not love myself, and my looks had, at this point, deserted me. If, like most people who have tried mirror work, you have come up against this, you know how difficult it is. It feels like a complete lie.

I am telling you, it gets easier.

Keep going, even if it feels like you are pretending.

I know this because of the opportunity I was offered: a "backdoor" to self-love. You can do this too.

I remember softening my gaze and letting my focus blur as I looked into my eyes. At some point, I began to see the stranger in a new way—as I would look at someone else. I could always show up for others, be and say all the right things, when they were in pain. I just couldn't do it for myself. I didn't yet feel worthy of that love as Brandi, but I could look at this other woman, this stranger with no hair and no eyebrows, a big round head, swollen cheeks, her entire body full of inflammation, and feel understanding, compassion, and gentleness.

I could feel the love radiating out of that person in the mirror, even though I couldn't feel it was me. And I began, unconsciously, to align with that frequency.

For so long, I had been trying to go back to where I was before. Back to when I was healthy, back to when I had hair, back to when I thought I had it all together. As I went through this process, I had to keep reminding myself not to compare this new version to the old, familiar one.

It wasn't until I completely embraced what I looked like without the covering that I really started to heal. Looking back, this was why I didn't like wearing the wigs—there was a yearning inside that I could not yet identify to shed the masks I had been wearing.

As I tuned in to the person in the mirror, the layers and layers of conditioned identity began to peel away. I had a visualization, similar to meditation, of the lagoon, and felt that same energy of being cocooned and loved. That's when, as I looked into my eyes and felt that unconditional love, I met my soul. I tapped into the remembrance of who I really am—not the personality or egoic experience of this lifetime, but my multidimensional essence, my spark of the Divine essence.

It was the death of the beauty queen that birthed the Light of the Soul.

This is how we learn to love ourselves and others unconditionally. To look at another standing before me and see their beauty, their vulnerability, and that raw humanness.

Self-forgiveness was also a huge piece of this. In understanding I was a creator spirit in a body and had been creating unconsciously, I was able to forgive myself for manifesting such illness and disease in this body. I didn't have the words at the time, but I did know that my ways of being and patterns and lack of allowing emotions to move through me had created an environment that was unhealthy.

This is not blame, but it is radical responsibility. This is looking at what we've created objectively and saying, "The level of awareness I had at the time led to the creation of the illness or some other circumstance. Wow, how powerful I am to have created that. Now, with this new level of awareness, I can create something else."

Suddenly, everything starts to make sense, and the judgment and the projection lessen. We begin to see how we're all connected and how we're all out here, creating ways to grow and expand in a variety of ways.

I cannot state this enough: *it is all about our current level of awareness.* No matter what has happened or is happening in your physical reality, increasing your awareness is where change occurs. The level of awareness changes everything, both in the manifestation of things in the first place and in your ability to move through them knowing you are being supported and guided—that you will always be okay.

> *Nothing about this journey is accidental or coincidental. Nothing is done "to us"; it is all done for us. I have been given the image of a corkboard, representing a lifetime on the physical plane. There is a red thread running through it, tacked to the board at certain "mile-markers" or junctures in our life that are the most significant for our growth. We are guided by Spirit and Higher Self to follow the breadcrumbs from one juncture to the next.*

I hate the word "tests," but sometimes that's the best way to describe them. They build strength and endurance. More importantly, they are building our capacity to hold Light in our physical form. We do this by raising our frequency … and how do we raise our frequency? We transmute the denser energy—fear, shame, and all resistance and judgment. We do this by feeling the emotions and moving them out of our body.

This is what I was doing while learning to love the "stranger" in the mirror, then accept and love her as myself. Emotions are just energy in motion. When we transmute them, those energies change form, allowing more Light, more joy, more fun, and more laughter to come in. And, because we feel differently (better), we begin to embody our higher frequency. The higher the frequency we hold, the easier it is to touch and communicate with Spirit. The key to this is maintaining that higher frequency so we can anchor in the Light and that frequency for everybody else.

When I make bold statements like, "I'm grateful for my illness and for feeling abandoned by everyone," I am not only speaking from the truth that I worked extremely hard to arrive at, I am also speaking with the utmost empathy, compassion, and understanding for those who are feeling stuck and alone in this moment. Helping others navigate this and learn to do it for themselves is my work as the bridge.

The abandonment by others during my illness highlighted the way I had been neglecting myself my entire life. The loss of my health and identity allowed me to begin shedding the masks I had been wearing my entire life. Most importantly, I learned my true self, the Higher Self, is always safe, and that I can always choose myself, no matter what anyone else does. And that is a security that cannot be taken away.

This is how we birth the New Earth.

PART IV

Ascension

We are living in a time of profound acceleration, when human consciousness is evolving at a pace never before experienced on this planet. The structures are shifting. The systems are unraveling. And the language we once used to describe spirituality no longer holds the fullness of what is unfolding.

Ascension is not about leaving the body or escaping the world; it is about embodying more of your light within it. It is the rising of awareness beyond fear and separation, and the return to unity, truth, and wholeness.

Much of what we've been taught has come through a third-dimensional lens, rooted in duality, hierarchy, and disconnection. As we awaken, we begin to see through those filters and remember: we are not separate from the Divine. We are expressions of it.

This chapter is not about arriving at some final destination. It is about integration.

Living in alignment.

Bringing the higher frequencies down into the body, into relationships, into everyday life.

Ascension isn't something that happens to us.

It's something we embody.

One choice, one breath, one moment of remembrance at a time.

TRANSITIONS AND TIMELINES

A t one point in this process, I saw myself as a "chosen one." I laugh at that now. I thought "ascension" meant I would leave this place, like, "I've evolved, I'm outta here, what's next?" I didn't know where I would go, just that it would feel good. There was definitely escapism energy around that.

Sorry, folks, but that's not it. *We actually lined up to come here and do this work.*

Yes, ascension is about movement, but not to another physical space. We are moving from the third dimension to the fifth dimension, which is a different level of awareness, all *while remaining in the body.* It's going from egoic awareness—"I'm just a person in a meat suit"—and experiencing the world through the five senses, to a heart-based awareness that experiences the multidimensional self and the interconnectedness of all things.

Notice I said a *different* level of awareness, not a *better* one. This is not about making the ego the villain of your life. The ego gets a very bad rap in our culture and especially in the spiritual community, but the truth is it's an aspect of self, and a very useful one at that. When we expand our awareness, we see the ego as a tool, helping us operate in the physical world. We can even learn to laugh at it when it starts trying to run the show.

It's a common misconception that only special people move through this and gain enlightenment. "Chosen" is an outdated term, and anyone still using it, or any other terms that express separation, polarity, or judgment, is simply showing you their present level of consciousness. *The truth: we are all spirits currently embodied.* We all have higher selves guiding our journeys, giving us "growth opportunities" to step into new ways of being. Anyone can do what I'm doing if they have the desire and take initiative and action.

How I *am* different is the speed with which I moved through awakening, especially considering how far I had to travel. From what I understand, most people do it slowly, even over decades. That's what we want, for the vibration and frequency change in the body is a lot to move through. The slower we go, the easier the process. It was as if after forty-five years on the ant farm, I was "sling-shotted" to another reality, and it has definitely been a bumpy ride.

As we expand, we pull back to see the ant farm from a higher vantage point. We can still have those physical experiences, but we can also see what is beyond them. We know more. We get more downloads. Another visual I love is one Sunny gave me, that of climbing a ladder to heaven.

When we have a third-dimensional level of awareness, we don't know anything above us. Yet our Higher Self is there, guiding us from the top of the ladder. As we do the work, embody more light, and ascend, we see the world around us—both the beauty and the illusions—in a new way.

The word "illusion" is one that's tossed around a lot, and it used to really bug me, which is to say it made my highly developed bullshit meter go off. Then I realized illusion is just another way of saying separateness from Spirit, from our Higher Selves, and from each other.

> *Words, regardless of their textbook definition, carry an energy that fluctuates depending not only on the lips of the speaker but on the ear of the listener. You might read something in this book that repels you now and changes everything in the future.*

Back to the ant farm. Like everything else, it is neither good nor bad BUT/AND it exists at a certain level of awareness and therefore involves a programmed predictability. As we ascend in our consciousness, we are able to take inspired action to move out of that predictability and step onto another timeline.

A timeline is simply the outcome that results from doing the same thing in the same way. When we do something to step out of that and step into the fear, we shake up the system. We move from reactors to cocreators.

It is important to understand that these steps do not have to be enormous leaps forward all the time. They can be something as simple as responding differently to someone than we normally would, with more love for ourselves.

For example, if we always agree to do something we don't want to do, and we start saying no, we are not only changing the dynamic of the relationship with that person, we are also changing our own trajectory. We are moving in the direction of enlightenment, even if the movement is so small that we cannot yet see it. And yes, this does mean we will have to disappoint others. This is okay, even welcomed and necessary for you and for the other person. You are inviting them to step into a new timeline and way of being as well.

Another common misconception is that after our one big awakening, we are automatically enlightened. Enlightenment is becoming our Higher Self. It is acknowledging that ladder going to heaven, with Higher Self standing at the top. It is the embodiment of the knowledge we are receiving into the physical body so it becomes wisdom.

Again, this is an ongoing process. We don't wake up one morning and say, "Laaa, I'm Buddha!" It is making choices from an open heart, every day. It is making choices of service while also being loving with ourselves. It is seeing the interconnectedness of all beings and having integrity, trust, and respect for everything because you have it for yourself. It is Divine bliss, brought into the human experience. It is the ability to hold our frequency and Light, which creates a ripple effect, making it easier for others to tap in.

If it helps, know that this is not your first rodeo. We have all done it in other lifetimes. The only difference is that this time, Earth herself is ascending and evolving alongside us. This brings both intensity and opportunity, as we're not only healing individually, but also contributing to a much greater collective shift.

Ascension is the energetic process of moving from awakening to enlightenment. This is happening on several levels: physical, mental, and spiritual, conscious and unconscious. We feel the Light and the energy coming to us; we are getting downloads of information.

At the same time, our cells, our very DNA, are changing from carbon to crystalline. This happens through an energetic process of embodying light codes in physical form. I compare it to my son gaining weight before a growth spurt.

We have life experiences that we move through and gain new awareness from. We open up to light and information that's coming down. Our body is electrical, so a lot is happening when the energy is moving. It's a slow, gradual process of moving through density and releasing it. Memories come up to be released, not pushed down into the box again. Our work is to look at it, feel it, and then move through it. This allows us to take in more Light, more knowledge, to realize more potential, and manifest more of what we desire.

First, though, we have to clean up all the shit we have accumulated while living in the 3D world and lacking awareness. By this, I mean living in polarity, competition, survival mode, and fear. This is what's often referred to as trauma. I really don't like this word, not because I am above it or anything. I went through one "trauma" after another from age three to forty.

I don't like the word because of its negative connotation and because it's been overused. The experiences we call traumas are actually growth opportunities, but before awakening, we don't see it this way. We don't realize that it's just energy, meant to move through us, and so we stop this movement. We put these experiences in a box, seal it with packing tape, and shove it in the back of the closet. When we do this, the dense energy stays trapped in the physical body and leads to the manifestation of physical diseases and conditions.

This also happens on a collective level. We, like the Earth itself, are raising our frequency and starting to see the systems for what they are. Externally, this manifests as people "losing their shit." And no wonder, when we are constantly bombarded with noise. The media is like a virus, only we can't avoid it by wearing a mask and social distancing. It's in our feeds, it's in our emails, it's the ad before we get to the video we want to watch. It keeps us off-balance, distracted, and feeling unable to trust our own discernment.

This is the fourth dimension, folks. It is that space where we see the puppet strings but have not yet fully realized where our power lies. That's all fine and part of the ascension process; what's happening, though, is that some people get stuck there, meaning they're stuck in blaming and pursuing "justice" from the perceived offenders. They dig their heels in. They cling to that "us versus them" mentality. They remain in separation.

> *No matter who someone is or how enlightened they claim to be, they will always reveal their true level of consciousness whenever they sit in judgment or use the language of separation.*

Ascension happens organically, through Higher Self and Spirit, BUT/AND we have to do the work. Awareness would not have become wisdom if I didn't put in the energy, intention, and self-love, and take action to move that energy through me. If we're going to be co-creators, we have to step up to the plate, period.

We ascend by opening our heart; it's how we move from 3D to 5D. My heart was like Fort Knox with armed guards around it. To open it, I had to commit to showing up for myself, taking care of myself, and trusting myself so I could build confidence. It was saying, over and over again, "NO MATTER WHAT, I WILL BE THERE FOR MY HEART."

In the fifth dimension, we see puppet strings and the puppet, and we laugh because it is irrelevant. We can also see where we have been in that place of resentment and victimhood. We see that in reality we have been co-creating the whole time because we didn't know, so we were pissed at ourselves. This is not self-blaming or shaming, but rather reflection, such as, "Oh, isn't that interesting …?"

If this sounds impossible, like some kind of pipe dream, or you just don't know how to get there, I understand, because I felt the same way. If you want to know how to get started, turn off the news and play either classical music or nothing. See how you feel then. Watch how fast you get hooked on the silence, on the whisper of your own soul.

Finally, this is an ongoing process. Similar to the myth of the "chosen people" is the misconception that awakening is a once-in-a-lifetime thing, that we go from giving the finger to the guy who cuts us off in traffic to chanting OM and hearing angels singing. Nope. There is no finish flag, no "I am almost there." We get many opportunities to awaken, and the ascension is a continuous journey of exploration, embodying more Light and gaining a higher level of awareness. It is loving more parts of ourselves.

Signs of Ascension

As we shift in consciousness and begin anchoring more of our Higher Self into the body, the process isn't always graceful or comfortable. Awakening doesn't just change how we *think*; it transforms how we *feel*, how we relate, and how we function in the physical world. These signs of ascension can show up as physical symptoms, emotional waves, sleep disturbances, or even a deep questioning of our purpose.

At first, many of these may feel like something is "wrong," but they are often evidence that something much deeper is aligning within us. Here are some of the signs I experienced on my path—and what they were trying to teach me.

Extreme Fatigue: This shift in awareness takes our life force energy. I had assumed my fatigue was due to Lyme and Epstein-Barr. Yes, they were part of it, but it was also the energetic process.

Sleep Issues: For years, I struggled with insomnia. What I didn't realize was that in that in-between state—where the body is still but the mind floats between worlds—I was receiving Divine information.

One night, in that semi-dream space, St. Germain appeared to me. He was surrounded by a deep violet light and what I now recognize as a merkaba—a sacred geometric shape of light. I visualized myself entering the merkaba, almost like stepping into a med bed for the soul. It felt like a purification chamber, elevating my frequency and accelerating my healing.

That night marked a turning point, not just in my physical body, but in aligning with my divine path. The next time you find yourself wide awake at three a.m., ask: *What am I being shown? What am I ready to receive?*

Pain: These are things like aching bones and joints, as well as stomach issues like nausea and constipation, due to the energy infrequencies in our body.

Emotional Sensitivity: I went through a period of huge releases, crying at memories that came up or just seeing a touching commercial. It felt like emotional whac-a-mole, and the only thing I could compare it to was being pregnant.

On the flipside, I also went through a period of detachment, which was far more disconcerting. It was not despair or depression;

I simply felt like I didn't care about anything at all. What I later realized was that I was moving away from enmeshment and trying to control and stepping into trust. What feels like isolation is us stepping back from people, places, and things because we're learning how it feels to have our energy back. We are not giving it away to just anyone or anything anymore.

Intuition: As your intuition shifts and toggles, you might experience brain fog. I was often unable to find words or express what I meant. Sometimes I felt like I wasn't "all there."

Purpose: As your Higher Self guides you to where you need to be, you might experience changes in your job, relationships, and where you live. Your work, which can be quite challenging, is trusting that they reflect your new timeline and your path for this lifetime.

These signs are not random symptoms or setbacks—they're evidence of your evolution. Your body, mind, and spirit are recalibrating to hold more light, more truth, and more of your soul's essence.

While the process can feel disorienting, even isolating at times, you are not broken. You are becoming. The key is to stay curious, trust what you're experiencing, and allow your inner wisdom to guide you through each shift. The more you honor what's rising—rather than resist it—the more gracefully you can move into alignment with who you truly are.

RAISING THE ANTENNA

The energy, or Cosmic Knowledge, that I tap into is available to everyone. The only difference between me and someone who "cannot" connect is that I learned to raise my frequency, my "antenna," high enough to meet that energy. That's when I realized it had been there all along, supporting, guiding, and nurturing me. It is doing the same for you, always.

The first few years after Awakening were a complete overhaul of my life on every level.

I was healing my physical body, following Steve's protocols to rid myself of toxicity and fungal overgrowth, visualizing myself as already well (which was a key component and often involved a lot of "pretending"), and incorporating movement into my daily routine.

At the same time, I was continuing to open myself to multidimensional energies in the "spiritual school" (the baths) and learning to reframe my past experiences from traumatic to opportunities for growth.

It was a beautiful and exciting time. I was insatiable in my quest for knowledge, both theoretical and experiential, about this new, vast world opening up to me. That first class with Sunny led to another, then another. I joined mastermind groups, listened to podcasts, and got intuitive readings. I tried every modality out there, from craniosacral therapy and acupuncture to gemstones and Reiki. (The last two,

I intuitively knew—or, to be more accurate, I "remembered" from previous incarnations—and would later use with my own clients.)

I had never studied or read about these things before, so I truly was able to embrace them with a beginner's mind. Every time I went out on a walk, I received these downloads of information. I didn't know they were downloads; I thought it was all me, and that I must be really, really smart! I felt dynamic and knowledgeable, as if I understood things in a new way. *That's good!* I would think when some insight or pearl of wisdom came to me, *maybe I should tell it to somebody!*

That said, this period was also incredibly overwhelming. I was managing my fear that the illness would worsen again. I was still navigating an ego death and learning to love and forgive myself. I was learning about my energy and my ability and right to invest it where I wanted, even if that meant not being all things to all people all the time.

It was a lot, and though I felt more clearheaded than I had in a long time, I often wondered if I was going crazy. Were these messages I received, often while taking my walks, accurate, or just wishful thinking? Was I just making all of this up?

There were times when I thought it would be easier if I were going crazy, then I could just take a pill and be done with it.

There were times when I thought it would be cool to check out of this circus altogether and hang out with the angels permanently.

Every time, I chose to keep going, even when it was hard, even when I thought I might always be sick, and even when I thought I might wind up walking this physical journey alone.

Because I kept going, because I kept putting one foot in front of the other, because I kept tuning out the noise of the world and going within, I was raising my frequency. I was raising my antenna, which allowed me to access higher vibrating energies.

At first, there was nothing intentional about this because I didn't know about intention, and an "antenna" was just something on an old TV set. It was more like I was stumbling upon these energies. Imagine swimming and rushing and "bumping" into different feelings and learning to recognize the individual signatures and who they belong to.

Along the way, Spirit gave me plenty of help in the way of breadcrumbs. Many were so subtle that I barely noticed them, or only realized in hindsight the opportunity I had been presented with. Others were so clear that it was as if I were being handed a miracle ... and indeed, I was.

In 2018, I was guided to attend a three-day spiritual conference featuring several well-known channelers and healers. I had come a long way in my development by this point, meaning I was consciously working on self-love, growing in my trust of the messages I received, and participating in Sunny's community.

Going to this conference would be another significant step forward, as I was going alone. I was demonstrating my faith in Spirit and my willingness to be my own backbone, rather than relying on others.

That did not mean it was easy. There were no self-congratulations, no, "Yay! I have got this awakening stuff worked out." It was more like I was sitting in a venue so huge I couldn't even see my comfort zone, knowing not a soul or what to expect. When the people on stage started doing things I'd never believed were possible—things like spontaneous healings—it was even more overwhelming. This person I was becoming (or, more accurately, remembering) was battling my inner skeptic for control. I had no idea who would win.

When one man asked those who needed healing to stand up, I heard what seemed like hundreds of chairs being pushed back as people got to their feet. I looked around as he then started to channel. Was I the only one confused here? How could this possibly work? How could he heal so many people with different ailments at once?

Definitely a WTAF moment.

I was aware of a woman standing up behind me. I don't recall what her situation was, but the healer started sending energy to her.

And, though I still didn't understand what was happening, I could feel the energy. It was almost like he was talking to her, but *it was coming through me*. I had never felt anything like it. I felt the tears coming, and I let them. I felt a healing.

The session came to a close right after, and everyone started filing out of the room. Not me, though. I remained seated, the tears still silently falling onto my cheeks. I didn't want to talk to anyone or do anything. I was just going to stay there until I felt ready.

Suddenly, I saw a heavyset Black woman approaching me.

"Can I hug you?" she asked, and as soon as I said yes, she embraced me and put my head on her bosom. It was beautiful, like being hugged by a grandmother.

"You are healed, child," she said. "You're healed."

She then turned and walked away, leaving me to wonder who she was and why she had come to me. Was she a guardian angel? I didn't know, I just knew there was a connection between us, and that I had just experienced something profound.

The next day, I boarded a plane bound for Thailand with my husband, Sunny, and some others in her community. I wasn't dismissing the experience at the conference—I knew better than that—but there was that slight feeling of, "Did I make more of that than it really was?"

Sometimes when we're in an experience, we know it is so powerful, then the ego steps in and tries to convince us otherwise. In fact, I had texted Sunny that night and told her I'd had a healing, only to regret it the following morning, thinking I had made it all up. Dennis wasn't aware of any of this, as I wasn't sharing my spiritual experiences with him at that time.

When the in-flight movie began, I asked for headphones and settled in. I didn't know what it was about, and I didn't much care. If you've ever been on a long flight—this one was about seventeen hours—you know you'll do anything to pass the time. Plus, it was based on a hugely popular book.

The movie was … drumroll, please … *THE SHACK*.

For those of you who don't know, it's about a man who is going through a years-long, extremely dark night of the soul after his young daughter is abducted. He goes to "the Shack," the location where her murder presumably took place, after finding a mysterious invitation in his mailbox.

When he gets there, he is met, not by the killer (he had suspected that person of sending the invitation), but the Holy Trinity: God, the Son, and the Holy Spirit. They help him begin to heal and understand that while we often don't see it through our human eyes, there is a Divinely guided and very intricate plan for our highest and best good.

As soon as I saw the woman who played God, I knew in my bones that I was being given a sign. And, no, folks, I am not suggesting that Octavia Spencer hugged me at the conference. But the physical similarity between the two women, so soon after I had expressed curiosity about what had happened, was absolutely a confirmation that the healing, the connection between me and this woman, and her words to me, "You are healed, child," was real. And then, as we so often do, I put that away and forgot about it. Thailand awaited.

That trip would indeed mark another milestone in my healing. One day, we went to a sanctuary to visit with rescued elephants. I can still remember the elephant's skin, rough and dry, under my hands, and the energy when I leaned in toward one and touched my third eye to hers. In that profound moment, I not only felt a deep connection with this magnificent creature, but the unity of all things.

It was also in Thailand that Sunny turned to me, gave me one of her knowing looks, and said, "You know, you're a teacher."

The hell I am, I thought, because the notion seemed as far out as the galactic reading I had gotten the year before. Thanks to Google, I now knew what "consciousness" was, but I didn't feel like a pioneer, and I certainly didn't think I had anything to teach others.

And, once again, Spirit laughed and said, "We'll just see about that."

JESUS AT THE BACKDOOR

Spontaneous healings are real and are possible for everyone. In most cases, however, physical and spiritual healing happens step by painstaking step, because each of those steps is so valuable to our soul's growth.

Somatic work was a significant step for me, and instrumental in that it helped bring me back into the body after a lifetime of escaping from it. As a result, I was better able to discern my energy and distinguish it from energies I was connecting with, and between one angel or guide and another.

This was how I met Jesus … except I didn't know it was Him.

I was blessed to work with Kate Shipp, a somatic trauma-informed practitioner and a dear friend. During our sessions together, energies often stepped forward to support and give me messages. One day, I recognized a presence I had been connecting with for some time. I knew little about him, though I had sensed from the start that he was different from the others, with incredible power and profound humility in equal measure.

He was also endlessly compassionate like Mother Mary and Kuan Yin (whom I had also felt), but, again, somehow distinguishable from them. I hadn't given this too much thought because I was regularly "bumping" into several energies.

His name, Yeshua, was one I'd never heard before and also seemed irrelevant. I was learning that angels and guides, including an energy who'd identified himself as Juan, were not interested in being given credit for their work. Who they were was not as important as what they were there to convey. We are the ones, with our human, third-dimensional awareness, who give them names and titles and put them into categories. We're the ones who need to make logical sense of it.

Imagine my surprise, then, when during the session Yeshua suddenly revealed Himself as Jesus.

"Why," I remember asking incredulously, "didn't you tell me who you were?"

His response: "You never would have believed the message."

No argument there. Had He come to me and said, "Hey, Brandi, it's me, Jesus!" I would have dismissed Him. First, I probably would have thought I was making the whole thing up. Second, even if I did believe, I would have rejected Him and His teachings.

The old programs would have immediately started running, reminding me of how isolated I had felt at my Catholic high school and the things I'd been spoon-fed there, for example, that everything is a sin, that in part led to my atheism. Jesus—at least the version presented to us by religious systems—comes with a lot of baggage.

More recently, I had experienced some behavior from churchgoing people in my area that seemed to me distinctly *unChristian*. Specifically, my son Dennis was excluded from sports and even shunned by a good friend because our family did not go to church.

This pissed off my inner Mama Bear to no end and reaffirmed my judgments about religions and their followers. Just the name "Jesus" was a tripwire of sorts—a symbol of the hypocrisy I was perceiving.

Of course, Jesus was well aware of how I felt. He was also undoubtedly quite used to people denying and/or mistaking His message for the rhetoric spoken in His name. This is why He had chosen to backdoor His way into my heart. Of course, I also had to play my part, which was to *open* my heart enough to feel that energy and let it in.

When Jesus came, I could, for a moment, see myself through His eyes. He was so accepting, loving, and gentle of every aspect of me, while also being strong and steady. In His energy, I recognized that familiar feeling of home that I had felt with my husband and Sunny.

Jesus also provided validation and reassurance that I had stepped into my purpose. For some time, I had been volunteering, first in Steve's healing communities and then with Sunny's. Much of my work was behind the scenes, and all of it was unpaid, which others in my life couldn't understand. "Like, what are you doing? That's not the way things work around here!" It got me thinking, *Am I doing all this because I don't feel worthy of compensation?*

This was actually a really good question to ask, considering the lifetime of unworthiness I was working on shifting. We should *all* be asking ourselves these kinds of questions about our work, our marriage, our kids, our friends, and so on. It is how we learn to distinguish between what feels good and what doesn't. It is how we recognize the choice points about where to invest our energy and when to pull it back, then act from a place of self-love. Our power lies within each choice point, and, by the way, folks, we get approximately *35,000* opportunities each day to exercise it.[5] It truly is mind-blowing.

Though I was fairly certain that I was following the path I was being called to, it helped tremendously that Jesus got it. He saw me; He reflected to me that true call to humble service because He had walked a very similar path.

So has Steve, who selflessly and tirelessly gives of himself to people in desperate need of guidance, with no expectation of receiving anything in return. I heard that ring of truth the moment I connected with him. Steve, I realized, carries an energy very similar to

---

[5] Amanda Reill, "A Simple Way to Make Better Decisions," Harvard Business Review, December 5, 2023, https://hbr.org/2023/12/a-simple-way-to-make-better-decisions.

Jesus. There are also parallels between my relationships with them—one was happening on the physical plane, the other on the spiritual.

Remember, this journey is never just happening on one level.

It was no coincidence that Steve—the person who ultimately played one of the biggest roles in my physical healing—offered his help completely free of charge. But I wasn't ready to receive that kind of support until I had first taken a leap of faith.

Before meeting him, I had to reach a point of surrender. I had to ask for help. That meant doing things I had never done before, like seeing a naturopath and investing money in my healing—something I'd always found hard to justify. It forced me to confront my sense of worth and deservingness, to begin allowing in an energy I had never really felt before.

If Steve had come first, offering help for free, I probably would've dismissed it. I needed to make the commitment to myself *first*. Only then could I recognize the genuine, heart-centered support he was offering—not transactional, not attached to an outcome. Along the way, I also encountered people who were clearly selling—pushing products or services with that heavy, salesy energy that never felt right to me. Feeling the discomfort of that contrast helped me recognize the purity of Steve's intention. His gift was never about money. It was about service, alignment, and love. And by that point, I was finally ready to receive it.

Similarly, before meeting Jesus, I had to do the work to raise my frequency enough to start sensing and communicating with multidimensional energies. I not only had to suspend my disbelief and learn to trust the information I was receiving, I had to ask for help from my guides, angels, and Spirit when I needed it and accept whatever form in which it was offered.

In both cases, I had to be willing to let go, not only of the conditioned thinking learned from systems—in this case, the medical and religious systems—but judgments of those systems themselves. This was neither a short process nor an easy one. It is one of mental and energetic expansion, or what's commonly referred to in "spiritual speak" as moving from the third to the fourth dimension.

As mentioned earlier, this is not a physical escape but a shift in awareness; the fourth dimension is not so much a dimension as a tunnel between the third and fifth dimensions. While in this tunnel, we have an expanded view of our world, which, to be honest, can not only frighten and confuse us, but really piss us off.

For example, when I first learned about doctors and the medical system, there was a lot of finger-pointing, judgment, and blaming, and for good reason. It was not just about my recent experience; it brought up wave after wave of the hell I had gone through from my stomach surgeries, not to mention what had happened to my mother.

I thought about all the people who had died and were dying needlessly, whether it was because they didn't have the finances or had plenty of money but no one to listen to them. I was angry about how close I came to being one of them and what that would have done to my family.

This was doubly so of my beliefs about religion, for I had held those for decades. While I am still not a follower of organized religion, I have let go of judgment. First, because when we sit in judgment of another (no matter the reason, including their judgment of us), we are in separation, which hinders everyone's expansion. Second, I have realized that for some, religion is an authentic way of connecting to Spirit and a pathway to healing. Jesus, whose energy is one of pure humility, love, and, above all, genuine, has been instrumental in teaching me this.

> *Your rage at injustice, in whatever form it takes, is justified, just as mine was. BUT/AND when we are pointing fingers, we are part of the problem. We are feeding it energetically.*

Each of us has a decision to make: stay in the fourth-dimensional "tunnel," or recognize it as a growth period and continue moving toward greater awareness, balance, expansion, and joy. It is choosing sovereignty over mental and energetic enslavement.

When I am able to maintain my energy, it doesn't matter what anyone else is doing, from doctors and preachers to gossips in my social circle, from talking heads on some political roundtable to the politicians they decide to trash or exalt. When I am holding a high frequency and level of awareness, I no longer feel the need to give my energy to any of it, because I know it's not important, period.

In all the times we've spoken, Jesus has never spoken about religion with me. In fact, His guidance during the awakening process bore no resemblance to any kind of dogma or rules; He certainly never divides people into the "saved" and "unsaved."

As someone for whom religion was an emotional tripwire, I can say this definitely allowed me to trust on a deeper level. As mentioned, He didn't even reveal His identity until I had been communicating with Him for quite a while (over a year, in fact). Instead, He allowed me to connect with Him in a different way. He held space, knowing and trusting that I would discover it for myself.

In much the same way, Steve never told me what to do; he never gave answers. What he did do was ask questions that made me think even deeper. He provided me with information that increased my level of awareness, then encouraged me to rely on my own knowing.

These are the hallmarks of a true teacher. Sunny, who has also been an incredible teacher for me, explained that this is far more difficult than one might think. All you want to do is stop another's suffering, but you know the best way to help is to share wisdom, then honor their sovereignty as they follow their own Divinely guided path … no matter what that path looks like from the outside. This is what I aspire to when teaching others.

This is what this book is about: planting a seed of awareness that develops organically for you as you learn to follow the breadcrumbs on your path. Can you and should you ask for help? Yes, that is part of this. We are not meant to do this alone. What we are meant to do is learn to tap in, trust, and rely on our Higher Self, which has been guiding us all along.

Over time, the presence of Jesus became a steady and loving support—part of my team of Light and a guiding force throughout my awakening. But what I've come to understand is that this presence isn't something *outside* of me. It's not about a man in robes or a figure in the sky. It's a frequency—a divine vibration of love, truth, and compassion that we all have access to. We can all align with it, if and when we're ready.

For me, He showed up in ways I could recognize, guiding gently, waiting patiently for the moment I was ready to understand His deeper involvement, not just in this book, but in my role within the greater collective shift. That clarity would come later. For now, I still had steps to take and breadcrumbs to follow.

TURNING DOWN THE NOISE

Throughout this book, we have been shifting our perspective to see every experience in our lives, no matter how painful it feels or negative it appears, as an opportunity to awaken and ascend.

Our individual experiences are a microcosm of what is happening in the collective. There are plenty of examples in our current reality—one of the most obvious being political polarization, with each side vilifying the other and everyone perpetually angry. Seen from an expanded perspective, we might recognize the media's role in manipulating the situation, do our own research, and choose unity over an "us-versus-them" mentality.

The most illustrative event, however, in recent years was the COVID pandemic. Yes, there was chaos, confusion, illness, and fear, BUT/AND, there was also an incredible invitation to press pause on the world, go within, and expand.

I am not saying it was easy. As in every situation, we had to accept this invitation despite the distractions vying for our energy—from learning how to navigate remote work to talking heads telling us how to think and feel.

My situation was similar to many: suddenly, everyone was stuck in the house, conducting their lives on screens. My husband was working, and Billy and Dennis were taking their classes, high school and college, respectively, online. It was a lot.

My health had vastly improved by this time; in fact, before the pandemic, I had even had the lap band surgically removed. As I mentioned, it never worked right, and since the prolapse that nearly killed me, it had been stitched to my stomach to keep it from flipping again.

I wanted that foreign object out of my body. I felt it was contributing to inflammation, and becoming strong enough for the procedure was a huge milestone in my physical journey.

Now, though I was continuing to heal, I was able to focus more on developing my relationship with Spirit, both in the bath and on my daily walks in nature.

That's when I felt guided to release the antidepressants I had been on for over twenty years.

The desire for this was twofold: these medicines, in particular, keep you at a certain set point emotionally, meaning they prevent you from going to the depths, but they also prevent you from elevating as high as you can. More importantly, I had a knowing that I did not need to be dependent on them to regulate my emotions.

This was not a sudden decision, but the result of years of healing on all levels, one level at a time. In the beginning, all my energy had to go to healing my physical vessel; then, I began to learn about—and focus on—healing the energetic body, energy healing, spiritual healing, and emotional healing. I did a lot of emotional work before I felt ready and prepared to release the pharmaceutical support.

My knowing that it was time to do this came after regularly connecting with Spirit and Higher Self to the point where I had learned to trust my guidance and follow the breadcrumbs They were placing in my path. I cannot emphasize enough how important it is for you to make decisions based on your circumstances and follow the guidance of your soul and Spirit team.

The most challenging part of this process was not giving up the pills, but having to work with a Western medicine psychiatrist to do so. As I've mentioned, over the past few years, my trust in this system, once absolute, had been shattered, resulting in a lot of fear, trauma, and a desire to avoid anyone involved in it.

However, the consensus was that I needed medical supervision while being weaned off the antidepressants. This included my current naturopath (I was seeing my third and learning a lot about their unique areas of focus), who would support me holistically while I detoxed.

I was being presented with a choice point: continue taking the medicine, which I no longer felt was serving me, or work through those denser energies and allow myself to be guided to a practitioner I could trust. (At this point, I had no relationship with a doctor around this; I just got my refill every six months.) As you are probably surmising by now, I chose the latter.

It was no small feat finding a Western medicine provider willing to support me and take on the responsibility. Not only had I been on these medications for nearly all of my adult life, I was also taking an ungodly amount of them: three hundred milligrams of Effexor, an extremely high dose for my weight, and two other medications.

In fact, I was repeatedly told I would never be able to do it. What they didn't understand is that after the experiences I had moved through, the word "never" was no longer in my vocabulary.

Tapering down was neither an easy process nor a quick one—it took more than six months and a lot of support in the form of vitamins, supplements, and nutrition. Those walks were also vital for my mental health, and it's important to note that in more than two decades, no one suggested moving my body and/or being in nature as an alternative to medication.

Once I was on that lowest dose, I never went back. Again, I had a knowing that it was time for me to be free of these medications that had come to feel like a cage. That said, I hold no judgment about it, and I do give gratitude for the support that got me where I needed to be.

As mentioned earlier, the psych evaluation had also yielded a diagnosis of Complex PTSD. This was partly due to the illness; however, it was greatly exacerbated by eighteen months of not being believed by others. Earlier experiences, such as what I witnessed, read about, and was involved with during my decade in enforcement, were likely contributing factors as well.

There was also the knowing that my brain wasn't working right, not in the psychiatric sense, but because of the parasites and bacteria attacking my system. Borrelia burgdorferi, the bacterium that causes Lyme disease, is a spirochete, meaning it has a corkscrew shape that enables it to swim through fluids. We now know that spirochetes also pass through the blood-brain barrier and interfere with your thoughts and emotions.

It's called "Complex" PTSD for a reason, folks!

I chose to look at this through a spiritual lens rather than a holistic one—meaning, I moved forward not with an organized treatment plan, but by following Higher Self's guidance on what I needed to do, organically, for my spirit.

These were all holistic and natural healing modalities—ozone therapy, saunas, Reiki, salt rooms, EMDR, tapping, NET—anything I could do to purge that energy. Spirit would send me to a provider, and their specialty "just happened to be" the next thing I needed, such as gemstone and frequency healing, to peel back another layer.

There are a lot of labels tossed about, like PTSD. I am not saying that these things don't exist. What I am saying is that they are not life sentences. We can heal through it. Here are some steps.

Acknowledge

The first step is to have awareness, meaning you identify and acknowledge whatever it is you're wanting to shift. In my case, I wanted to shift the energies of being sick, and not being believed about that sickness.

Share

Regardless of your circumstances, feeling heard is a *huge* piece of this. You need to move the energy, because as long as it's in your body, it will still carry a charge. Writing is a great way to move energy out of the body and channel it into something else. I have written so many letters to my body, and my body has written many letters to me. Every time, this communication caused me to move that energy.

The best way I have found, however, is to express with your voice. The first time I went to Dr. Yosef, I was there for over an hour. He allowed me to share my symptoms, what was happening to me and what I *thought* was happening, how I felt, and what I was afraid of.

I healed more in that hour than any other, because for the very first time, somebody listened to me, and I felt complete. I felt hope. Yes, I needed the treatments too, but they might not have worked, at least not as well as they did, if I hadn't felt heard.

Who you tell is not as important as their ability to hold space for you without judging, correcting, or advising. This is why coaches, mentors, and communities are so important.

Ground

Tapping into your creativity—be it painting, writing, knitting, or whatever you're drawn to—is incredibly healing for the body, mind, and spirit. To do so, however, we first need to get into the body.

One of my favorite tools is the camera on my iPhone. I have always loved photography, and focusing on my subject has been excellent for bringing me back to the present and to stillness.

When we look through the camera's lens, we pull away from the ant farm and view the world from different angles and perspectives. This is also a very practical tool, because our phones are always with us. While creative activities are not a substitute for acknowledging and sharing our experiences or feeling seen and heard, they are extremely healing and add fun and joy to the process.

For a lot of people, this is when resistance comes up. They do some of the work, then they don't want to feel anymore, so they push the emotions down again. The thing is, the body remembers, so when they inevitably get "poked" again, that energy comes back up. They are back at square one.

> *This is not about judgment. If you find yourself at square one, the most important thing is to release any shame around it. You cannot get this wrong. Healing and connection are waiting for you, whenever you are ready. Whether you are at square one or find yourself back there, the first thing you need to do is be present, to be in your body.*

The good news is that we no longer have to rely on talk therapy to do this work. We can choose that if we want, and there's still value in it, but there are so many other ways, like NET, breathwork, and the other modalities I have mentioned, to move and transmute that energy. These serve as backdoors, allowing us to push the ego aside and get right to the energy to move it from our body.

When a pattern comes up and you feel "poked," recognize with gratitude that it is an opportunity to expand beyond that pattern. You can react with the programmed response, or you can pause and ask yourself, "What would love do?" or "What would self-love look like?" For one, self-love would express how you feel and hold boundaries.

Make an Intention

We are creator beings, working with energy every minute of every day to attract things into our lives. This is happening whether we realize it or not; the key is to consciously choose to focus our energy on what we desire. The energy needs direction from us, the creator beings, to know which way to move.

When we set an intention, we move from waiting and reacting to creating and taking action. This can be incredibly scary in the beginning because we are taking complete responsibility for our lives. It's realizing we are the captain of our own ship and always have been. It brings up our history and times when we might not have guided that ship in ways that felt good. That's why we have allowed the media and others outside ourselves to make decisions for us.

For me, it brought up all the times I promised myself I would work out or lose weight or do something else I knew was good for me, only to break those promises. I had trained my body not to trust me, and now I had to build that trust. I had to step into a new way of being.

You can too.

If you find it difficult to even form an intention, asking yourself questions can be incredibly helpful. I have often asked myself, "What does that three-year-old girl inside of me need?", "What does my body need in this moment?", and "What do I need to hear?" For example, you might want to hear that you are safe and/or that you are loved.

Whatever it is, ask, and know that you can be that for yourself.

Each time we pause, ask ourselves what we need, and then follow through, we learn to trust ourselves. We become more confident. This is a journey of 100,000 steps, so set yourself up for success.

Also, don't forget to acknowledge the progress you have already made. This is what led, albeit unintentionally, to #movemybody30. Per Sunny's request, I posted a photo of myself walking on what I *thought* was the Facebook page for the private mastermind group I was part of.

When I realized I had posted on the *main* Facebook page, with over a thousand people, I was mortified. First, I was much more comfortable behind the camera; second, I felt a bit silly, like, "What's the big deal? Anybody can walk for thirty minutes." But the truth is, not everyone could do it in that moment—certainly, there were years when I could not have done it.

That post turned out to be a celebration of me showing up for myself in a way I had never done before, *and* it became a movement within Sunny's ELEV8 Your Light, inspiring others who were working to build that trust with themselves. I continued #movemybody30 for a year and a half, and, again, it was vital for my mental health during the pandemic and detoxing from the medications.

I cannot emphasize enough the power of the mind to affect our environment and our body. If you are not currently able to move physically, you can, through visualizing this movement, create a profound healing.

> *When we believe the body can heal itself, trust that it has what it needs within, and follow that guidance, we unleash one of the most powerful forces in the Universe. We rewrite our script. We make the impossible possible.*

In 2023, after seven years, my hair grew back. This was two years longer than Spirit had originally told me, but I kept believing. During that time, I had learned the lesson to love myself, with or without the beauty queen's golden curls, and my external reflected that inner vibration back to me.

Choosing the Right Community

I cannot say enough how vital community was for my healing, on every level. Initially, I joined online groups for people dealing with Lyme disease and autoimmune illnesses. They helped me learn about the science behind these diseases and ways to heal them; just as

important, they let me know I was not crazy and alone. They would also present me with choice points about where I wanted to put my energy and what timeline I wanted to follow.

Let me explain.

We attract experiences and people that are vibrating at the same frequency as us. The same is true with communities. When we don't understand how energy works, we can confuse support and trauma-bonding. One facilitates our growth and expansion, the other can perpetuate the patterns we want to leave behind.

Clearly, learning to distinguish between the two is critical. The question is, how?

First, you learn your own energy. You do this by turning down the noise and connecting to Higher Self through meditation—whether it's in the bath, walking in nature, or whatever works best for you.

Next, you learn how to distinguish it from the energy of others, including family members and others in your closest circle.

You have already had moments of this. It is the feeling you get when you walk into a room and sense tension among others. Once you're aware of where your energy ends and others' begins, this sensitivity becomes more consistent. You're more tuned in and aware of what others are feeling. You can even start to feel plants and animals, as well as the difference between higher- and lower-energy emotions.

It also becomes much easier to discern when you are disconnected and/or numbing out. It can be as simple as washing dishes and thinking about what you're going to make for lunch. This is not a bad thing. We are simply expanding our ability to take in higher energies, and that takes time.

I learned a great deal about discerning energies from the online communities I joined. While working with Steve, I started facilitating some of the groups in his community.

Initially, it felt good to help others; however, I quickly realized that my body felt drained after spending time in those groups. I wasn't consciously saying, "Oh, I am learning how to discern the energy of the community." I just knew that when I got off the calls, I didn't necessarily feel better; eventually, I even started to feel some dread and resentment, which was confusing because I really did want to be of service.

It wasn't until I started working with Sunny that I began to understand. One day, after I had shared with her what I was feeling, she replied, "Well, why don't you give yourself a break?"

"What do you mean?" I asked. "I am helping people."

She told me, plain and simple, that I couldn't keep doing this. I was taking on the energy of illness and holding it in my body. Though I was still conflicted about what to do, I listened to what she was saying. I wanted to be able to act from a place of self-love, as she did.

As soon as I sent the email to Steve telling him that I needed to take a step back, I felt lighter. It was as if I was setting down a heavy backpack I didn't even know I was carrying. I also took all the updates out of my feed so I wasn't constantly being bombarded with illness. After a week or two, I felt better.

Bottom line: we are here, first and foremost, to master self-love and raise and maintain our frequency.

In time, I came to realize that, yes, while I truly cared and wanted to help, I was also still getting external validation by doing so. I was coming, not from my spirit, but from my ego.

What's more, I understood that the people in the groups had not been draining me; I *felt* drained because I had unknowingly been absorbing their energy. As always, this experience had several layers; I was not only learning this for the sake of my health, but so I could eventually step into my purpose as a teacher and hold space for others, no matter what they are going through.

You may also find that you expand beyond a community. We are all meant to grow and change, and if you are hanging onto people, places, and groups out of obligation and expectation, you are not making room for the new groups and experiences that Higher Self and Spirit want to bring in.

During those years, I was also guided to become more involved with Sunny's community, which was a completely different experience. Like Sunny herself, it immediately felt like home.

Here, I connected with women and men who were also exploring their spiritual gifts and doing the ascension work that allowed them to experience their lives from a higher perspective. It is no coincidence that this community had a very maternal energy that I had unknowingly been lacking my entire life. They provided a safe, loving space for me to start expressing about my spiritual experiences. By holding space for me, without judgment and without taking on my stuff or trying to fix it, they were teaching me how to do the same for myself and my family.

Were there heavier times, when some members were going through something challenging? Of course. The difference was that we were all committed to looking at ourselves, being curious, and growing, rather than trauma-bonding. I especially loved the way we gently called each other out by asking, "Well, have you thought about that …?" I also noticed that those who were not vibrating at the same frequency did not stick around.

Communities, like individual people, are a reflection of you, and that's okay.

Sunny's communities continued to be a spiritual home for me, allowing me to be of service in a way that filled me up, first as a volunteer and ambassador to the ELEV8 Your Light membership community, then, over the past several years, working with Sunny and her team.

These experiences, such as creating mentor and cheerleading programs and managing a group of volunteers, were very much stepping stones, growing my confidence around holding space for others.

I then moved into teaching classes—something I never thought I would do!—leading meditations and speaking on gemstones, ascension, and other topics. Now that these initiatives, begun during the pandemic, are functioning independently, we are free to spread our message on a grander scale and reach more people in the spiritual university, School of Light (SOL).

We are the space-holders, placeholders, and frequency-holders, opening portals for others to walk through. The effect of this ripples all over our world, making it easier for everyone to embody and integrate these higher frequencies.

JESUS RIDES SHOTGUN

Wherever we land on the spiritual spectrum, the idea of Jesus, or more accurately, our *perception* of Him, can either become a stumbling block or a stepping stone.

For some, His name has been used to divide: to separate the "saved" from the "unsaved," to judge, to exclude. For others, it's not about the historical figure at all, but about the *frequency* of unconditional love, truth, and compassion that He represents.

That frequency isn't outside of us—it's something we can awaken within. In my experience, this inner presence began to surface and guide me long before I understood what it was.

It is all about baby steps.

This is why, as mentioned earlier, what I now recognize as the Christ consciousness within me communicated for over a year before I was ready to receive its full truth. Even then, it came in the form of Jesus, who announced Himself during the somatic session, because that's what I was ready to accept at my current level of awareness.

If that awareness had come too soon—framed in the language and imagery I was conditioned to reject—it would have shut me down. I had to move through my discomfort, my resistance, and my judgments before I could fully recognize and embody the energy I was being called to align with.

I came to understand that it is not about Him, but the Christ Consciousness energy He embodied, which is just another way of saying Light, unity consciousness, unconditional love, expansion, truth, and humility.

This is precisely why I chose to wait until now to reveal Him as the Divine energy who showed up in my car on the highway that day. I wanted you to have your own experience with the information contained in this book without any preconceived notions.

At that time, I was already close to completing the writing process. It was, for the most part, the story you have read here: my experiences and learnings before, during, and after Awakening and Ascension.

While I knew my expansion would continue, I envisioned the culmination of this book to be the trip I had taken a few months earlier, when I walked the Camino del Santiago with Sunny, other members of the community, and Dennis. It had been a major milestone in my healing and embodiment work; it also symbolized my journey to self-love and inner reliance.

When I boarded the plane for Europe in September 2024, I wasn't sure what to expect. Certainly, the rigorousness of the trip was on my mind. The terrain on the Camino can be quite challenging, and, as you know by now, I was no stranger to navigating physical limitations. Though I had been healing for years and felt really good, I wasn't at all sure I was capable of something on that level of difficulty. I also knew it was supposed to be a spiritual experience, but for the last several years, *every* experience had been spiritual.

On both counts, it turned out to be far more profound than I could have imagined—not only a true testament to my body's resilience in the face of all it had endured, but a turning point physically, emotionally, and energetically. I hiked a total of sixty-two miles, nineteen of them in one day, something I would have never believed possible even a year ago. It was as if I had closed a cycle, one that had begun when I couldn't get out of bed without pain or fatigue, and when I thought I might never wake up at all.

When I returned to the States with that experience so fresh in my mind, I decided I would begin the book with Camino and circle back to it at the end. Both the walking and the writing involved the shedding of another layer of skin; each had informed and nurtured the other. It made sense.

Jesus threw a wrench in that plan in the best possible way. During our conversation, I came to understand what is happening in the collective and my role in it. Why He decided to do this while I was trying to avoid the wildly weaving vehicles on the freeway? Well, I had a few ideas about that.

For one, driving has generally been a great time for me to connect. My body and my thinking mind are engaged in the business of physical life, and Spirit can slide right in.

For another, there was absolutely no chance of my doubting the experience when my personality self was hyper-focused on avoiding a crash. Spirit does, at times, have a flair for the dramatic.

Finally, there is the simplest answer of all: *Jesus appeared when I specifically asked Him to, because I needed Him BUT/AND, He was also reflecting the frequency at which I was already vibrating.*

Of course, several other things were happening at the same time, on different levels, all of them Divinely Orchestrated. In fact, I realized that Jesus had been sending me signs of something big for a while. At the same time, I had been doing my part, upleveling my embodiment work so I could hold more Light in my physical form.

For several months before the Camino, I had been going to Aaron Eliserio, a practitioner I was guided to, for a form of body work called fascial release. As we move through challenging experiences, many of us unconsciously grip, brace, or armor ourselves, and that energy gets stuck in the body. In other words, "our issues are in the tissues."

Body work, particularly fascia release, teaches us how to soften into safety through conscious touch and embodied trust practices. Aaron was the first practitioner with whom I felt safe to be touched without dissociating; this allowed me to learn to connect to my Higher Self while in the body to find out what I needed. As a result of this work, I began losing weight with more ease and grace than ever before.

The Camino had also been a significant piece of my embodiment work.

Finishing our leg of the walk was a true moment of victory over every self-limiting belief I had ever held. I felt like I had crossed some dividing line between the first half of my life and the second. I was walking the talk—literally!

It felt like a sacred milestone in my relationship with Dennis. For the first time, I truly allowed him to see me in the role of teacher, and he met me there with such love and grace.

I'll never forget hearing him share with Sunny and others how proud he was of me. That moment touched something deep in my heart. It was the fruit of years of inner work we had each done, both individually and as a couple.

Yes, I had sparked a turning point with that 2019 letter, declaring how I intended to show up for myself and our family, but Dennis *chose* to rise alongside me. I am profoundly grateful for his openness, his devotion, and his willingness to walk this path of expansion with me. From the very beginning, I knew he was the one. To be his life and soul partner is one of the greatest honors of my journey.

When he told me after our trip that he had felt his dad, who had recently transitioned, walking with him, I was in awe. And yet, something about it felt beautifully natural. The man who once spoke with wonder about galaxies and star systems was now embodying that same cosmic connection in a whole new way—stepping into his own awakening. We're growing, evolving, and remembering together, and for that, my heart is full.

Yes, we had always loved each other BUT/AND it was our commitment to authenticity and expansion that not only saved our marriage but completely transformed it.

Shortly after the Camino, I was given another invitation to engage in more embodiment work. I had continued to shed weight (overall, I lost one hundred pounds, forty of them over the last several months), and I was very happy about it. Why, then, did a friend's innocent comment that I was getting "so tiny" bring up discomfort? It was, I realized, the residue from decades of feeling unsafe in my body. Suddenly, being surrounded by a very tall husband and German shepherds, while wonderful, was also a mirror, reflecting my need to feel protected.

This is how it works, folks. I was aware of the feeling. I looked at it from an expanded perspective and asked for help by talking with Sunny about how I could feel stronger in my body.

Her suggestion of muscle-building exercises seemed like a good way to go, as did having an accountability partner since this was not something I had seriously done before. Aaron, my fascial release practitioner, was also a personal trainer, and since I already had that comfort level with him, I booked a session. I did not expect to enjoy it. If I'm being honest, I thought I was going to hate it.

Not only did I not hate it; I loved it. Aaron was the perfect trainer for me, and I almost immediately started feeling and seeing the results in the form of increased muscle definition and strength. We also did a lot of work around mobility and flow, which contributed to my feeling of groundedness and overall well-being. Of course, this wasn't without its challenges.

When Aaron told me he was going to have an offering, I told him I was happy to make a post promoting him. He had been taking lots of photos of me, which he used to better check my form, so I asked if he would send me one to use for the post.

That night, I had just gotten into bed when my phone pinged with a text from him. I opened it, expecting a photo, and instead saw a full video of me doing arm curls while on one of those mini trampolines. My immediate reaction? I threw the covers over my head! The best part was that I was home alone.

Yes, friends, I was hiding from *myself*.

A key ingredient in ascension work is the ability to laugh at yourself. When I was done doing that, I started asking, "Okay, what is going on with me right now?"

I also acknowledged, *without judgment,* that I needed some time before watching the video. I said, "Isn't this interesting …" which completely shifted the energy from one of shame or embarrassment to one of curiosity. It invited expansion.

That's when I understood that working with a trainer wasn't just about getting in better physical shape; it was about overcoming my fear of being seen. I knew I was going to be sharing this on social media, and it was hard to be so vulnerable about my body. For you, it might be difficult to be vulnerable about something else. It's the same feeling, and you just have to push through it.

It was Divine and perfect, and exactly what I needed for my growth, which, over the last year in particular, seemed to be happening at an accelerated rate. Throughout the book, the Camino, the weight loss, and workouts, I was feeling more and more comfortable teaching classes and sharing my story. I was feeling more comfortable in my skin.

And then the pain started—excruciating pain down the side of my neck and into my scapula. It was not unfamiliar (I had first felt it at age sixteen, and at that time was diagnosed with fibromyalgia), but it hadn't happened in several years. And if that wasn't enough, I got shingles, also very painful, and had pretty severe pain in my tailbone.

Pain is awful, no matter when and where in the body it happens, but when you've suffered with a chronic and/or life-threatening illness, there is also a fear that's triggered. The human part of us is saying, "What is this? Is it connected to what I had before? Is it coming back?" At least, that's how I used to feel.

This time, I leaned into it and asked, "What is my body trying to tell me? What is it trying to release?" That said, I also "yelled" at Jesus a bit, basically demanding to know why I was going through this when I had done SO much work on myself, physically and spiritually.

Knowing that tailbone pain was related to the root chakra and therefore my sense of safety and security, I went to a practitioner, recommended by Aaron, for myofascial sessions to release that energy. Part of the natural healing arts (it's somewhat similar to chiropractic), it involves manipulation to restore balance in the body. He performed what's called "thrust joint manipulation" to pull out my tailbone. Myofascial work releases energy accumulated in the joints, so after the session, he told me to soak in Epsom salt.

I hadn't taken a bath in that sacred space in a very long time, but as soon as I got into the water, I was right back there. Suddenly, all the angels and guides came marching in on both sides of me. At first, I thought they were letting me know of an upcoming funeral, but when I asked what it was, I heard, "Graduation!"

I had no idea what the hell that meant, but at least it didn't sound like anything to be frightened of.

That same night, while in meditation, Jesus validated what I had sensed by showing me an image of the shack, from the movie of the same name, that I had seen on the plane to Thailand years earlier.

Immediately, I recognized this as a full-circle moment. The "graduation ceremony" indicated that I had crossed some kind of threshold, and the shack was a message that the Holy Spirit was with me.

The physical pain continued for weeks, and as I was working through it, I heard about and felt guided to take a three-day online class about connecting with Jesus. The teacher was one I held in very high esteem. Her journey was very similar to mine, and she had posted about it, providing "real-time" validation, back when I was not yet comfortable sharing with others and needed to know I was not alone. When a mentoring session with Sunny, which had fallen during class time, was rescheduled, it seemed a confirmation for me to attend.

The first day of the class, the teacher opened the space and invited Jesus' energy in. Though I had an experiential learning and was grateful for it, I found myself (the personality self) a little disappointed. *I already know how to connect with Jesus*, I thought, *I could probably teach this class myself.* There was some sadness behind those words, because in the past, I would have felt filled up by it.

Yet, that class is what prompted me to call Him in in a new way, while I was in the car.

"Are you ready, Brandi?" He had asked. "Are you ready for what's coming?"

The human part of me wanted to say, "Uhhh, you're going to have to be a bit more specific about that ..."

Instead, I heard myself saying, *"Yes, I'm ready. I trust."*

I had finally arrived in a place of complete surrender.

Three times, at different points in my journey, I had heard a voice asking me the same question, though it was phrased more like, "Are you done? Have you had enough?"

The first time was in 2012, after all the lap band surgeries, including one that almost ended my life. The second was a few years later, after breaking my foot, and the third was in 2017 or 2018, when I was starting to recover from the illness.

In each case, I had no idea who or what was asking me, or what they meant. It was disconcerting for sure, especially the first two times, when I had no spiritual life but had been gaslit around my mental health. Was I being offered some kind of "exit plan"? Was I going crazy?

By the third time, I was much more curious. Was this an angel? A guide? It was only now that I recognized that energy as Jesus.

His question had become clearer as my awareness expanded.

"You," Jesus told me, "are going to be rewriting scripts."

Throughout this book, I have been talking about what I call *Purification of Perspective*, which is humanity turning off autopilot, breaking free of this control matrix, and stepping into Truth. We have *always* been the creators of our reality, individually and collectively. We have *always* had the energy. We've *always* had the power, and we still do. We just forgot.

When we, through Awakening, start remembering this and start doing the work, we are learning to embody Christ Consciousness. More importantly, we, for the first time in human history, can embody this energy and become Ascended Masters while in a physical body.

He is talking about a complete paradigm shift.

This shift is already happening. The Earth and everything on it is already expanding at an accelerated rate. We are already seeing the foundational problems, the way we are being controlled by systems. Jesus is speaking to the masses who get stuck in that middle space, that fourth dimension, where they see this and give their energy away instead of continuing to expand and seeing the bigger picture. That means that instead of finger-pointing and judging each other, we ask, "What are the gifts in this situation? How can I raise and maintain my frequency? How can I break through?"

I was also reminded that this is nothing new. The turmoil we are seeing in the world has happened countless times before in different forms. And, as always happens, things are going to continue to be uncovered and revealed about these systems.

This is very similar to what happened during Jesus' physical life. Consider the massive paradigm shift His message created, and continues to create, in the world. Think of the barriers He faced in creating that change.

Some chose to remain invested in the systems and continue to operate from a place of fear and control. They knew that if others began seeing through Jesus' eyes and started creating from Unity and Freedom and Truth, those systems were going to fall away. They wouldn't be needed anymore. And yet, through humble service, He rewrote the trajectory of the human experience.

Now He wants to do it again. My work is to help people rewrite their scripts (and therefore their timelines) as I have rewritten mine, so that they can embody the Light we are all made of and embrace unity consciousness, not when we transition, but now, here, on Earth.

This is the real meaning of what's referred to as the "Second Coming." This is what Jesus meant when He said, "I am the way and the truth and the life."

CONCLUSION

I have often joked that Spirit has to trick "human Brandi" into following my path; for example, when I posted my #moveyour-body30 photo on a Facebook page with a far greater reach than the one I intended. This not only forced me to be more vulnerable but also allowed me to help a larger group of people, just like others' posts have helped me countless times along the way.

This book is no different; I began writing it with the intention of sharing my spiritual awakening through an illness and the ascension process that followed and continues to this day. While this is still true, it has become so much bigger than that.

That illness was not just happening in the physical. It was a battle for my soul. At any point, I could have chosen to stay in a lack of self-love; I could have chosen to stay on the ant farm, in a place of separation from, and judgment of, myself and others.

This is not about giving myself a pat on the back; it is about telling you that if I can do it, so can anyone.

We. Are. ALL. That. Powerful.

This book also accelerated and deepened my journey in ways I never anticipated. There is a reason it's called the "writing process," for in the telling of this story, I have also been purging its energy from my mind, body, and spirit.

As I processed it, Higher Self and Spirit gave me information that allowed me to understand those experiences from a higher level of awareness. This was all divinely guided and coincided with the closing out of several cycles in my life, some of them that began in childhood and came to the forefront during the illness and my healing process.

Some, like my pilgrimage on the Camino and working with a trainer, closed out cycles of not feeling safe and strong in my body. Myofascial release work has allowed me to release and transmute residual energy stuck in my tissues, which made it possible for me to embody more Light and hold the frequency needed to communicate with Jesus at the level I did in the car that day.

> *In other words, my physical vessel had started to vibrate at the same frequency as I was internally.*

Other events took me completely by surprise; most were joyous, a few were frustrating; one brought me to my knees emotionally. All were an invitation to expand further and reaffirm my commitment to becoming as enlightened as I possibly can while still in this physical vessel.

Jesus assisted me in clarifying this purpose: I am here to help others do the same by rewriting mental scripts that have kept them imprisoned in the ant farm. This includes scripts that keep us reliant on anything and anyone outside of ourselves, even God and Jesus Himself.

> *Jesus has no desire for, or investment in, our dependence on Him. We are told many stories about Him, one of which is that He sacrificed His physical life to "save" us from our "sins." What He did was show us, through His ability to embody the energy of unconditional love despite what was going on in His physical environment, that we can do the same. We are made from the same Light. We can be "ascended masters" while still in the physical body.*

Anything outside of us is a 3D concept that attempts to understand the nature of unity consciousness or the creator. Whenever we focus on a singular source—GOD—it can lead to the perception, often seen in religions, that we are separate from the Creator and others who believe differently. This causes judgment and prevents us from recognizing the Creator in all of us.

It is the same when we try to categorize and label angels, ascended masters, and multidimensional beings. Certainly, it allows for deeper and more diverse energies to be experienced and appreciated, but the reality is that, like us, each aspect represents a unique vibration that is part of the Creator.

Drops of water in the ocean make up the ocean.

In doing this work, I am merely facilitating the ascension that is already happening, at an accelerated rate, on the individual and collective levels. We all have expansion work to do for this to happen; however, when we do, we are also healing the scripts for those who have passed and those who have not yet incarnated.

Let me explain.

I have written at length about my mother's lack of self-love, both its contribution to her passing at a young age and its impact on me for most of my life. So, when I received that message after she transitioned that "I did it for you," I assumed she meant that she was teaching me how to love myself.

Later, when asking Spirit and my Higher Self why I was going through this very challenging journey, I heard, "For Billy." At my level of awareness at that time, I assumed this was referring to all the advocating I had done on his behalf. These interpretations were true, BUT/AND, they were also just pieces of a larger picture.

It wasn't until a recent meditation that I understood the full significance of what was happening. I saw in my mind's eye a set of Russian nesting dolls, each one representing an ancestor—my mother, my grandmother, my great-grandmother, and so on—I was helping to heal. In transmuting my pain and lack of self-love, I was helping them do the same.

At the same time, I was showing Billy, whose journey has been similar to mine with regard to both challenges and spiritual gifts, that living without masks is not only allowed but essential to reaching enlightenment.

Together, we explored the myriad gifts people with ADHD possess—those of creativity and visionary leadership; an intense focus on projects they are passionate about; charisma and vitality; and heightened compassion, empathy, and intuition.

At age fifteen, he had a full kundalini awakening and is embracing his unique gifts.

Now twenty, he has recently indicated that he is ready to start teaching spiritual classes. Imagine how many people he will help and the ripple effect he will create over his lifetime!

We are doing the hard work and paving the way for those in our energy field to step up and open the door with more ease and grace. Yes, they still have to open the door, but we have done most of the heavy lifting.

At the same time, one of my greatest teachers was preparing to transition out of his physical life. Dax, a German shepherd, joined our family four months before I broke my foot and six months before my mom died. During my illness, he became the reason I forced myself to get out of bed when every movement required great effort. For years, I told the story that he had saved my life.

It wasn't until recently, when Dax became ill and I was doing everything to save him, that I realized the burden I had projected onto him. It was much like the responsibility my mother projected onto me to carry her emotionally.

Animals are so often seen as cute companions that bring comfort and joy into our lives. While this is true, they are also highly evolved, sovereign, and sentient beings who have their own journey of soul expansion and their own purpose, usually to hold a mirror up to and teach their humans.

Dax's purpose was not to save me; that was *my* work. His purpose was to shine a light and show me what unconditional love looked like so I could give it to myself. There was also physical mirroring happening; Dax was having problems pooping, and I was having pain in my tailbone, both of which involve the root chakra, or our safety in this physical world. Our animal companions are always absorbing our energy, always showing us what we need to lean into or release.

I have always had a challenge maintaining my frequency around animals I perceive to be in pain or discomfort. At one point—and though the thought of losing one of my dearest and most loyal friends was unbearable—I came very close to ending Dax's suffering.

What I realized, with the help of Sunny and trusted animal communicators, was that I was really trying to end my feelings of not being able to withstand it. I was being called to be a sacred witness of his journey, just as I am with the humans in my life. In that moment, I was able to release Dax from his obligation to me; later, when he indicated that he was ready to transition, I was able, albeit with much sorrow, to let him go.

During Dax's physical life, our energy had been completely enmeshed and entangled. He had absorbed into his body all the energy that I, at my current level of awareness, had not been able to transmute: breaking my foot, my mother's passing, and my illness.

When he dropped his body, he took his energy with him, which freed both of us. When I tap into his frequency now, I understand that he can now be an even better support because I am ready to transmute that energy—one of very deep grief—he'd been holding.

There is no end date to this journey, folks, no end to the learning. We are infinitely expanding, continually balancing our human self with our Higher Self, so we can embody the Christ Consciousness within this physical vessel. This is often painful and hardly ever comfortable, but as our awareness increases, it becomes easier and more joyful.

Sometimes, it's even funny.

I was recently reminded of this one afternoon when, while sitting in the backyard with my husband and Billy, an owl came to visit.

This began a "conversation" that lasted nearly four hours.

It's no surprise that communicating with animals is different from conversing with other humans. An energy exchange is *always* taking place, but when we speak with people, we rely on their words, tone of voice, and facial expressions.

With animals, much like with angels, galactic beings, and crossed-over loved ones, we have to be present and really feel into their energy to understand what they're communicating.

There I was, talking with my family while also feeling into the owl's presence. It was one of calm, reassurance, steadiness, and protection, yet, though I knew he had a message for me, that "something was up," I didn't know what it was.

As we were having this exchange, our son Dennis texted that he was planning to ask Payton, his long-time girlfriend, to marry him. Detailed plans and pictures followed. His excitement was palpable, and my husband and I were so happy and proud.

We've had the gift of watching our son grow into a strong, thoughtful, and resilient man. In middle school, he faced painful bullying, which only deepened his empathy and compassion.

In high school, he became class president and wrote a powerful college essay about overcoming judgment from his local religious community—an essay that helped earn him admission to the university of his choice.

As an adult, he rose from project manager to vice president in just four years, leading with integrity, heart, and vision. Now, he's beginning a beautiful new chapter with a woman we deeply admire, and we couldn't be more proud.

And yet, there was that owl, still hanging about, still trying to tell me something I couldn't quite grasp. And, as the minutes, then hours, ticked by, the human me went into programmed fear. My family was traveling abroad the next day, and I was aware of having some concern, that waiting-for-the-other-shoe-to-drop kind of energy. Was the owl coming with a warning? Should we not be traveling? He had been awake all afternoon, which is unusual for owls—was that some kind of omen?

The messengers and their signs keep coming, and it comes down to how present we can be in this world. When we're worrying about the future, we are not grounded in the present; therefore, we cannot understand the message.

I knew I needed to get to a place of surrender and stop pestering the owl. Once I did, I was able to relax and enjoy the beautiful day, talk with my husband, and watch Billy play with the dog. I relaxed into gratitude for that incredible moment, and the owl was just a part of it.

It wasn't until a hummingbird almost flew into my face and nearly startled me out of my chair that I realized, *Oh my God, it's Mom, and she's celebrating Dennis' engagement with us!*

Once I had awareness of that, I could laugh at myself, not in judgment, but with grace and compassion. It is often harder for me to connect with my mom's energy because, although our connection is closer in some ways than it was when she was here, I still miss her. And when I miss her, I'm not feeling her. The owl was there to tell me she was celebrating Dennis' engagement with us; the hummingbird was her way of "whacking" me over the head with the message because I wasn't getting it.

There are many signs of progress, but one of the biggest is when we find the humor in our experiences. It's an indicator that you are embodying more Light, and thus more joy. I also had a moment of amazement because I used to toggle between timelines; now I am living on one timeline but having multidimensional experiences within that timeline. In that case, I was engaging with Billy, playing with my dogs, and being proud with my husband, while also talking to an owl.

This is already happening to all of us. We are both participants in and sacred witnesses to the birth of the New Earth. We, embodying more of our Light, are the "second coming" that Jesus promised.

In closing, I would like to share a message recently shared with me by Hawk Spirit.

You are being reminded to rise above the noise and view your current path from a higher perspective. Like the hawk, you are a visionary—able to see the unseen, to sense the shifts before they arrive. Trust in your ability to discern the next right step, even if the road ahead feels uncertain.

You are at a symbolic crossroads. The numbers and names of the streets carry meaning too: 91 breaks to 9 + 1 = 10, a number of completion and new beginnings. Lejos means "far away," a sign that the journey you're on may be taking you to places not yet imagined.

The hawk says: "Do not fear the distance. Your wings are strong. Trust your inner sight. The path ahead is yours to claim."

Stay attuned. Stay elevated. And know that Spirit has placed this messenger before you not by accident, but to confirm you are exactly where you're meant to be.

I am here for this. I am devoted to this, body, mind, and soul. I am ready.

The question is … are you?

"TRIPPING OVER BREADCRUMBS"

by Dennis Strieter

I was enamored with Brandi from the moment she came into my retail store to buy some sunglasses. She was the friend of a friend, a spicy, spunky blonde who had a look of intensity in her eyes that matched my own. That's why three short months later, after a whirlwind courtship (and maybe a dare), it felt totally normal to call her father from a Las Vegas-bound plane and ask his permission to marry her.

I'll never forget the words he said to me: "Are you sure you know what you're getting into?"

Well, I can confidently say, twenty-eight years after we said our vows in the Little White Wedding Chapel, that no, I had absolutely no idea what I was getting into by marrying Brandi.

Never did it occur to me that our life together would be anything but perfect. We are both extremely driven, motivated individuals and, in my mind, NOTHING could stop us. Our family expanded with the birth of our first son, Dennis III, and that's when our journey to find ourselves began in earnest. We now had a new life to care for and, as all parents do, we wanted the absolute best for our child.

While I knew and understood many of the foundational stories Brandi shares in this book, I only identified with them tangentially, as events of another life, before I, The Great Provider, arrived. Deciding that none of that would happen on my shift, I disconnected from those feelings of her trauma and relegated them to the past. Our marriage experienced challenges, sure, but from my perspective the ectopic pregnancy and our difficulty with fertility were just signs that we weren't supposed to have another child. I grew up as an only child, and while it would have been exciting to have a brother or sister, I felt like I had turned into a well-adjusted adult. As I put my head down and got to work providing for the family, I was unaware of the profound effect these experiences were having on Brandi as a continuation of her journey.

I remember when we became pregnant with Billy, how happy we were that after six years we had finally conceived (you see how I conveniently leave out the child we had lost?). We also made the difficult decision for Brandi to stay at home, foregoing her career so I could focus on mine. When the shooting at her office happened, we literally "dodged a bullet" and leaned on that to justify our decision. According to my ego, we were untouchable. Bad things happened to other people because they didn't work hard enough to make them not happen. (Horrible, I know.)

Billy's developmental challenges were my first glimpse into a mirror that reflected an image of myself I didn't want to see. We didn't know what ADHD was, how to manage it, or what it meant for the future of our son. We just knew that Billy wasn't like our firstborn. He didn't seem to care for the same things, and he certainly wasn't put on Earth to please us by trying to fit some idea of what we wanted him to be. Instead, Billy was our great teacher, placed in our family at precisely the right time to guide us in finding humility and grace for each other.

Then came the injuries and illness. When Brandi broke her foot and her mobility was compromised, I focused on serving her physical needs and picking up the household tasks she couldn't do. I've always been the type to serve and excellent at keeping it all together, so even though her foot wasn't healing we looked to outsiders like we were thriving. That's what I was doing, folks—rather than addressing the issues in our family, I was "covering for them" through perceived extra effort.

If you've gotten to this place in the book, you know quite a bit about me. What you don't know is that when I was nineteen, years before I met Brandi, I was engaged to be married. During that relationship, my fiancée and I were in a motorcycle accident that resulted in her suffering a closed-skull head injury. For about ten days, she drifted in and out of a coma as the pressure from the swelling of her brain was reported on a red LED monitor. I kept vigil, spending every waking moment by her side as her body slowly healed. With injuries like this, many of the body's executive functions get reset or entirely disabled. When she came out of her coma, she was a different person, with different needs and different wants. I took on the role of caregiver, attending to her every need, going to every doctor's appointment, every PT and OT session, as she learned to walk, talk, speak, and love again. I also became the task-doer in our relationship. Everything she needed, I was there to help with.

After a few years and countless medical and therapeutic tasks later, she was able to resume a normal life. Our relationship, on the other hand, did not survive. Being so intimately involved in her recovery had transformed me from a mate into a caregiver.

Throughout this ordeal, I was completely beholden to the treatment modalities and practices that Western medicine prescribed for her. They were the experts, and you follow their protocols, period. This was my baseline when Lyme presented itself within Brandi. As I had all those years earlier, I went to every doctor's appointment and every treatment... and when they told me that there was nothing wrong with my wife, I chose to believe them. I had done my own research and there was literally NOTHING on the internet about all the co-infections she was experiencing. The few articles that were there indicated a psychological problem, not a physical one.

I wanted to go back to our early marriage, when we were two intense souls charting whatever course we wanted, in whatever way we damned well pleased. However, unlike Brandi's broken foot, I couldn't just pick up the extra tasks and give the appearance of normality. Nothing about what was affecting Brandi was normal, and no matter who we saw (I stopped counting after the third doctor told us there was nothing wrong. Brandi summarizes this when referencing "Dr. Birkenstocks"), they attributed it to a personal decision that she was making to be sick. I deeply regret the choices I made, and it pains me to recall my behavior during this period. I focused solely on working and was away from home on business much of the time, which perfectly fit the narrative that my wife was just looking for attention, not really sick. In my mind, this was a stage we were going through, not a marriage-threatening situation, and certainly not a life-threatening one.

Are you seeing a pattern here? I was becoming a caregiver, not the partner Brandi needed.

Through my lens, what was happening to Brandi and her multiple illnesses was mirroring what happened to her mother in the decades I had known her before her transition. Sherri was always sick with some type of malady that caused her to miss family events, vacations, and generally compromised her enjoyment in life. I took that to mean that this was how my wife's health would also play out. I thought that "eventuality" was what Brandi's father meant when he said, "Are you sure you know what you're getting into?" that October night when I whisked Brandi off to Vegas to elope.

My wakeup call came when her hair started falling out. Clearly, she wasn't "pretending" or doing this to herself. It was also not something I could fix through "extra effort." Our relationship was in a dark space during this time, not because we didn't love each other, but she could no longer TRUST me to always do the right thing for her. I had enmeshed myself with my wife, taking on the stoic role of provider and protector, and when I couldn't fix her by doing what the doctors told me, I thought myself to be broken. I am a guilty participant in our codependent relationship, never allowing Brandi to have her agency over her life. As painful as it's been to acknowledge, Brandi's loss of faith in me was the catalyst that allowed us to break this cycle. In fact, it was absolutely necessary for both of us and, ultimately, led us back to harmony in our relationship.

Humans love to look back at history and define those seminal moments where everything changed, for good or bad, and forever altered everything thereafter. In our story, the turning point was her diagnosis. It took ONE doctor looking at the totality of her journey, all of the co-illnesses, all of the previously attempted treatments, and finally declaring, "You have chronic disease caused by the bacteria that causes Lyme." It was on this day that Brandi finally and definitively could define and confront the enemy she was to defeat. From my perspective, this diagnosis gave Brandi the validation she needed from "outside her trusted source" (which at the time was only me) that she was, in fact, completely sane. Lucky for us, that was the only crack the Light needed to make its way in.

At this point, you know how the book ends, but in many ways our adventure together is just beginning. Yes, we continue to heal together though love, honesty, service, and Light; however, I also know I will learn a great deal more from Brandi as she fulfills her role in helping others awaken to their power during this time of "The Second Coming." I can't wait for the next lesson!

You see, through this journey and her illness, Brandi not only healed herself but showed me the framework in which I and our children can heal ourselves as well. I refer to her as "a puzzle that will take me a lifetime to solve," and it has been my honor and my greatest gift to walk this path alongside her. It is my hope that the lessons in this book resonate throughout your life, enabling you to find—and follow—your own trail of crumbs into the Light.

In service and gratitude,
Dennis

CONTINUE THE JOURNEY

I f you've made it to this point in the book—thank you. It's been an honor to share this part of my journey with you. Whether you found yourself nodding in recognition, shedding a few tears, or simply feeling something stir within you, I want you to know this: you're not alone, and you were never meant to do this work in isolation.

This book isn't the end; it's the beginning of your next chapter. If you're ready to keep going, I'd love to share some sacred spaces that have supported my own healing, awakening, and embodiment, and that I now help hold space within for others.

Visit My Website

You can learn more about my current offerings, workshops, classes, and private sessions at brandi@brandistrieter.com. I share tools, reflections, and upcoming events that support you in embodying your light, healing deeply, and expanding into the next version of yourself.

Meet Sunny Dawn Johnston

Much of what I've shared in these pages has been inspired, expanded, and supported by my long-time mentor and dear friend, Sunny Dawn Johnston. Sunny is a world-renowned spiritual teacher, psychic medium, and author who has helped thousands of people reconnect with their intuition, heal grief, and awaken to their soul's purpose.

Sunny has been one of the most important catalysts in my trans-formation. Her mentorship has changed my life, and I'm honored to now serve alongside her in supporting others.

Visit schooloflight.biz to learn more about Sunny and her work.

Explore the School of Light (SOL)

If you're feeling called to dive deeper into your own healing, intuition, and spiritual growth, I invite you to explore the School of Light, a heart-centered online institution of spiritual learning created to support you in awakening, embodying your truth, and living in alignment with your highest self. Founded by Sunny Dawn Johnston, the School of Light is where I now serve as an SOL Igniter, Faculty Member, and Community Ambassador, helping welcome, support, teach, and guide members on their unique paths of transformation.

The School of Light offers:

- Live classes, meditations, and breathwork journeys
- A vibrant, supportive community of like-hearted souls
- Access to teachings from Sunny and other incredible faculty
- Opportunities for deep personal healing and empowerment
- Heart-based business and leadership programs for lightworkers and soul-led entrepreneurs

This is also where you'll find ELEV8, the transformational membership that has become my home. It's where I awakened, where I healed, and where I found my soul family. ELEV8 is a space of deep personal growth, heart-opening connection, and powerful remembrance. If you're seeking a place to land, be witnessed, and rise in your truth ... this is it.

Whether you're just beginning or ready to deepen your practice, the School of Light offers a sacred space to learn, grow, and remember who you are.

Visit schooloflight.biz to explore upcoming offerings.

A FINAL NOTE

I 'll never stop being amazed by what happens when we choose to show up for ourselves. When we say yes to healing. Yes to truth. Yes to our own becoming. If this book lit a spark within you, I hope you'll continue to follow it. Your healing, your remembering, your *becoming*, it's all unfolding in divine timing.

Trust your path. Trust your Light. And know that I'll be cheering you on every step of the way.

With deep love and gratitude,
Brandi

ABOUT THE AUTHOR

Brandi Strieter is a spiritual teacher, intuitive guide, Reiki Master, gemstone healer, breathwork facilitator, and energy medicine practitioner. Her work weaves together mind, body, and spirit to support deep healing, soul alignment, and spiritual awakening.

After a long and painful battle with chronic illness, including undiagnosed Lyme disease and a lifetime of trauma, Brandi experienced a profound awakening that transformed every aspect of her life. Through her healing journey, she came to understand the power of energy work, self-love, intuitive development, and Divine remembrance.

Today, Brandi supports others in reclaiming their wholeness, truth, and sovereignty. She serves as a Faculty Member and SOL Igniter within the School of Light—a heart-centered online institution of spiritual learning founded by Sunny Dawn Johnston.

In her teaching role, Brandi offers experiential classes that blend energy medicine, embodiment practices, intuitive tools, and transformational healing. Through community engagement, she cultivates connection, fosters interaction, and helps bring the SOL community together with warmth, authenticity, and intention.

Brandi is known for her grounded wisdom, compassionate presence, and ability to create safe and sacred spaces that foster deep connection and transformation. Her teachings are rooted in lived experience, and her greatest joy is guiding others to remember and embody the Light that has always lived within them.

She lives in Arizona with her husband, Dennis, and their family, including her beloved German shepherd, Daisy. When she's not teaching, mentoring, or sharing her heart through writing, you'll likely find her walking in nature, receiving intuitive nudges, or engaging in mindful movement to stay grounded and strong.

You can connect with Brandi, explore her offerings, and join her in community at:

schooloflight.biz
brandistrieter.com

ACKNOWLEDGMENTS

To put this journey into words has been one of the most vulnerable, healing, and liberating experiences of my life. This book was written from my soul, through my body, and with the support of so many hands and hearts along the way.

To Dana, my editor and the one who helped me give voice to this story, thank you for walking this path with me. Your intuitive insight, presence, devotion, and willingness to step into new ways of being helped shape this book in a way I could never have done on my own. You were divinely placed on this journey with me, and I'm forever grateful.

To my publisher, Shanda Trofe of Transcendent Publishing, and Mary Rembert, thank you both for your thoughtful editing, insight, and care. Your ability to hold the heart of this story while helping refine its voice has been a gift. I'm deeply grateful for the heart and care you poured into every step of the process.

To Sunny Dawn Johnston, my mentor, sister, soul guide, and mirror. You have walked beside me through the most transformative years of my life. Thank you for seeing me, holding me, and reflecting the light when I couldn't find it on my own. Your example and your unconditional love helped me come home to myself.

To my husband, Dennis, your belief in me, your steadiness, and your own willingness to grow have been the soil in which so much of this healing has taken root. Thank you for standing beside me, especially in the mess, and loving me through every version of who I've been.

To my sons, Dennis and Billy, you are both my heart, my grounding, and my greatest teachers. Watching you grow into the men you are today fills me with hope. Your presence has anchored me, challenged me, and reminded me again and again of the power of love and resilience.

To my family and friends, thank you for the lessons, love, and reflections that have brought me here. I am grateful and blessed. Every part of our journey has served a purpose.

To Team SDJ, the ELEV8 and School of Light communities, my mentors, teachers, and soul family—thank you for walking this path with me. You've taught me that healing doesn't happen in isolation; it happens in connection and community.

To my beloved German shepherds, Dax, Duke, and Daisy, thank you for your unwavering love, protection, and presence. Each of you has helped me stay grounded and anchored in the present moment, reminding me what it means to be fully present and deeply loved.

To the doctors, healers, and every soul who shined their light and shared their gifts, thank you for helping me remember who I am and guiding me back to my own truth.

To Hannah Lorsch and Slate Media Creative, thank you so much for seeing me and capturing my light.

And to the seekers, those whose hearts feel the call, even when they don't yet have the words. This book is for you. You're not alone. You never were.

With a full and grateful heart,
Brandi

More Praise for *Breadcrumbs from Spirit*

It truly is amazing how God works. Sometimes the paths we take, the illnesses we endure, and the people we meet may seem like coincidences, but I've learned there's no such thing. Brandi and I were not placed in each other's lives by accident. Our meeting was perfectly orchestrated, guided by Divine Intervention, and it became clear from the very beginning that her healing journey and mine were meant to intertwine.

Like Brandi, I too endured a chronic, mysterious illness that brought me to my knees. I knew the heartbreak of going from doctor to doctor, only to feel invalidated. I knew the sting of being dismissed, even by people I loved. I knew what it was to feel trapped in a body weighed down with symptoms.

What I didn't know then was that this experience would become one of my greatest teachers, something no medical school could ever provide. In hindsight, it was a blessing in disguise, a breadcrumb from Spirit! It shaped me into a better doctor and gave me deep compassion for Brandi when she came to me because I immediately recognized not only her pain and suffering, but also her unwavering faith and surrender to Spirit. Though our journeys looked different, it was a bond that united us from the start.

The same frequency-based medicine that restored my health became the foundation of my practice and, in time, the bridge that carried me to Brandi. Our paths crossed through divine breadcrumbs—colleagues, connections, and timing that could only be explained as Spirit's hand at work.

When Brandi finally sat across from me in my office, I already knew she was someone extraordinary! Even in her suffering, she radiated joy and warmth. Her smile lit up the room.

Yet physically, her body told a very different story. She had lost all of her hair. Her body was swollen and puffy. Painful lesions and rashes covered her scalp, neck, and arms. Even as her body bore the scars of years of illness and struggle, she carried herself with strength and courage.

From the very beginning, Brandi shared that she was about 80% better, not by chance, but because she had already put in the work. She had refused to settle for defeat. She found Spirit, leaned into divine guidance, showed up for herself day after day, and did the hard work of healing, which demands so much: time, commitment, patience, resources, faith, and an unwavering will to keep going even when it would be easier to just give up. Though she had come so far, she was nowhere near ready to stop.

The process we began together was not quick. Healing at the root level never is. It often takes months, even years, of steady commitment. Many patients struggle to stay consistent. But Brandi was different. She showed up faithfully, followed through, and trusted the process. Her discipline, paired with her faith, became a powerful force in her healing!

At first, the changes were subtle—a little more energy, a softening of brain fog, brief moments of clarity. Yet even in the subtlety, Brandi chose trust. And in time, the miracles began to unfold.

Her skin lesions faded. The swelling subsided. Her head, once tender and boggy, began to clear. I will never forget the day she looked at me and said, "Dr. Danie, I believe that with your help, one day I will be able to grow my hair back."

After years of baldness and scalp pain, that moment finally arrived. Nearly two years into our work together, Brandi sent me a picture that stopped me in my tracks: she was smiling, beaming—with soft, beautiful new hair. I wept happy tears!

Brandi's healing, however, was never just physical. Yes, we worked on detoxing and supporting her body, but she also stepped into the tougher work—the kind many patients never dare to face. She opened herself to healing on every level: physical, emotional, mental, and spiritual.

She confronted her deepest traumas, released old patterns, allowed herself to be vulnerable in ways few ever will, and leaned fully into Spirit's guidance. In doing so, she fought not only for her health but for her true, authentic self.

Most people don't realize that the physical body is only one piece of the healing puzzle. Brandi did, and I believe that is why her healing was so profound! She discovered that putting herself first was not selfish, but sacred: an act of honoring her God-given worth.

As her doctor, I had the privilege of witnessing the resilience, courage, and faith that carried her through. As her friend, I was honored to walk beside her, rejoicing in her breakthroughs and cheering on her progress!

True healing is never the work of one path or one practitioner; it is the weaving together of body, mind, emotions, and spirit. Brandi embraced them all, and in doing so, she became a living testament to what is possible when unwavering faith and steady discipline are surrendered into Spirit's hands.

Brandi has now done something miraculous: she has taken her story—raw, honest, vulnerable, and beautiful—and placed it in your hands. *Breadcrumbs from Spirit* is not simply her memoir; it is a beacon of hope! It is a living testimony that the darkest nights can birth the brightest dawns, that pain can become purpose, and that every breadcrumb Spirit leaves is leading you home.

With *Breadcrumbs from Spirit*, Brandi carries the torch forward. A torch lit not by one moment, or one person, but by the many breadcrumbs Spirit placed along her path: the teachers, the tools, the faith, and the relentless work she herself put in. And now she extends that light to you, helping to illuminate your own journey.

If you are holding this book, it is no accident; it is a breadcrumb! Perhaps you, too, are searching: for healing, for meaning, or simply for the reassurance that you are not alone. Let Brandi's story be that reassurance. Let it call you back to the breadcrumbs Spirit scatters along your way.

May this book feel like a holy invitation, a call to trust your body, trust your Spirit, and walk the sacred trail laid out for you. May it remind you, again and again, that you are worthy of healing, wholeness, and the radiant life already unfolding.

Brandi is one of the most genuine, kindhearted, beautiful, and loving souls I have ever met. I am deeply honored to have been one small breadcrumb on her journey, and even more grateful that through this book, she now becomes a breadcrumb for you!

With gratitude and unconditional love,
Dr. Danie Brutocao
Naturopathic Medical Doctor

I am blessed and fortunate to have been in a position where I was able to help many chronically ill patients in their journey back to optimal health and wellness. This is one of the most rewarding aspects of my life, and I am most grateful to G-d that I was given this opportunity in this lifetime.

One of the most important things that I have learned from the many years of seeing patients in my private practice is the art of listening. I don't mean just listening to their complaints and physical symptoms, although obviously that is very important as well. I mean listening to their stories because everyone has an important story to tell. It is not always easy to truly listen in the short time that we have available during a consultation, but I try to encourage a patient to find their true voice and spirit, which often becomes suppressed when dealing with chronic illness.

Listening means that I always try to make space for the person that is in front of me while remembering that he or she is experiencing his or her own, unique journey and that often, the physical and mental symptoms that they are experiencing are tied to deep emotional and spiritual imbalances.

The current healthcare paradigm teaches us that we must FIGHT dis-ease; we FIGHT diabetes, we FIGHT Lyme disease, and we FIGHT cancer, but I think that this is an incorrect, fear-based approach. It is evident that this approach is not effective as the rates of chronic illness are soaring in the United States.

We tend to forget that in the process of fighting a chronic illness, we lose sight of the message or the opportunity that we are given to recreate ourselves and to realign with our true soul purpose. I believe that every single person has a unique, divinely orchestrated purpose and that whenever we steer off our intended path, circumstances will lead us to a place where we are forced to slow down our busy life and to reassess the current path in our life journey.

And so it was that somewhere along Brandi's journey to optimal health and realigning with her soul purpose, Brandi and I crossed paths in my office several years ago. Brandi's kindness and resilience were evident in her eyes when we first met. Her spirit seemed indomitable despite the physical challenges that she was facing.

The wonderful, beautiful Brandi that you see today may look very different on the outside when compared to the Brandi that was struggling with chronic illness a number of years back, but her radiant spirit remains unchanged. I am thrilled that Brandi made the commitment of honoring her higher purpose and decided to not only write this book, but to also dedicate her life to empowering others who are facing similar challenges to the ones she once faced.

I stipulate that one of the key factors in solving the current chronic illness epidemic is not only by encouraging more doctors and health practitioners to empower their patients during their journey back to optimal health, but also by encouraging patients who are able to free themselves of the shackles of chronic illness to find their voice so they can empower others by sharing about their journey.

I see this book as an inspiration to all, particularly to those suffering from chronic illness. Brandi's wisdom and intuitive insights acquired through her experience of dealing with chronic illness can be a great tool for helping others navigate through difficult facets in their journey. This book will help them see their illness as an opportunity for positive change, growth, and achieving their true divinely inspired purpose.

This book is also a testament to the resilience of the human spirit: It has the divine potential to raise a person from the lowest depths and elevate her to the highest places. My wish is that more people like Brandi will have the strength and resolve to choose to embrace their experience with chronic illness in order that they will not miss the opportunity to grow and to fulfill their divine purpose and be a source of light and inspiration for others in times of darkness.

Sincerely,
Isaac Yosef, NMD